P9-CEY-452

SCHOLASTIC

YEAR IN SPORTS 2014

SCHOLASTIC INC.

If you purchased this book without a cover, you should be aware that this book is stolen property. It was reported as "unsold and destroyed" to the publisher, and neither the author nor the publisher has received any payment for this "stripped book."

Copyright © 2013 by Shoreline Publishing Group LLC

All rights reserved. Published by Scholastic Inc., *Publishers since 1920.*
Scholastic and associated logos are trademarks and/or registered trademarks of Scholastic Inc.

No part of this publication may be reproduced, stored in a retrieval system, or transmitted in any form or by any means, electronic, mechanical, photocopying, recording, or otherwise, without written permission of the publisher. For information regarding permission, write to Scholastic Inc., Attention: Permissions Department, 557 Broadway, New York, NY, 10012.

ISBN 978-0-545-56259-1

10 9 8 7 6 5 4 3   14 15 16

Printed in the U.S.A.   40
First edition, December 2013

Produced by Shoreline Publishing Group LLC

Due to the publication date, records, results, and statistics are current as of August 2013.

UNAUTHORIZED: This book is not sponsored by or affiliated with the athletes, teams, or anyone involved with them.

CONTENTS

Seasons in the Sun!

As you prepare to dive into another awesome edition of the ***Scholastic Year in Sports***, let's take a glance at the past year of sports seasons to see what's in store in the pages ahead.

Fall is the first season in our year of sports, packed with the most popular sport in the country: NFL football! Relive the great games of last season and meet the heroes who made the memories: **Joe Flacco**, **Colin Kaepernick**, **Drew Brees**, **Adrian Peterson**, **Calvin Johnson**, and many more. And when the leaves are turning colors, the colors of college football are blooming around the land. Heisman winner **Johnny Manziel** had a great run, but the repeat success of the Alabama Crimson Tide was the biggest story of this season.

Winter brought snow and ice, and this year brought new stars to the winter sports scene. American skier **Ted Ligety** did something that hasn't been done in 46 years! Flip to page 169 to find out what. Canadian skater **Patrick Chan** took advantage of home ice during the world skating championships. And what about hockey? Why didn't the NHL start playing until January? Find out on page 104.

Spring springs into view as the boys of summer (that's what you call baseball players) get their mitts and bats out of storage. While the new season got under way, we took a look back at the 2012 World Series. Check out the scores and highlights, thanks to **Pablo Sandoval**, **Buster Posey**, and the Giants. Plus say hello to a new Triple Crown winner and good-bye to an all-time great. And what about the Dodgers' amazing rookie **Yasiel Puig**? Can he keep it up?

March Madness comes in the spring as well, and that annual college hoopsfest provided the usual amazing string of games. Who ended up on top? Find out on page 76. Spring is also when the NBA heated up . . . in more ways than one! **LeBron James** and **Tim Duncan** led their teams to the NBA Finals (again!). See how it all turned out on page 88.

Summer saw action sports galore, as the X Games traveled the world skating, riding, flying, and thrilling! Fans in four countries saw amazing performances, and you can read all about them starting on page 136.

Soccer kicked its way into the headlines in the summer, too, as the Champions League in Europe drew fans from around the world. The U.S. men's team battled to earn a spot in the 2014 World Cup, too, led by the return of star **Landon Donovan**.

And then it's time to do it all over again. The seasons and sports keep coming, and we come back every year to make sure you don't miss a moment.

Minnesota's Adrian Peterson came within a few yards of a single-season rushing record.

MOMENTS IN SPORTS
SEPTEMBER 2012 ▶ AUGUST 2013

The sports year in 2013 must have felt sort of left out. After all, 2012 had the Summer Olympics *and* a huge European Championship in soccer. But while 2013 didn't have world-spanning mega-events, it provided sports fans with tons of memorable moments.

If you liked football, you saw record-breakers galore in the NFL and repeat champs in the college game. If baseball was your sport, in 2012 you saw a very rare hitting feat and a Giant win, while in 2013, you watched the swan song of baseball's greatest closer.

Across the pond, tennis fans finally saw their long-held wish come true, thanks to **Andy Murray**. Sadly, on the other side of the ocean, a tragedy overshadowed one of America's oldest and most famous races.

The games went, and hockey fans were thrilled not only to see their teams finally back on the ice, but to watch a thrilling Stanley Cup final. The Blackhawks struck twice to snatch the Cup from the Bruins.

Finally, atop the sports world in popularity, viewers, and fun, the Super Bowl was number one. Did we get all of your top moments on our list?

And after you read these, start looking for next year's biggest sports moments!

10

9

8

7

6

5

4

3

2...

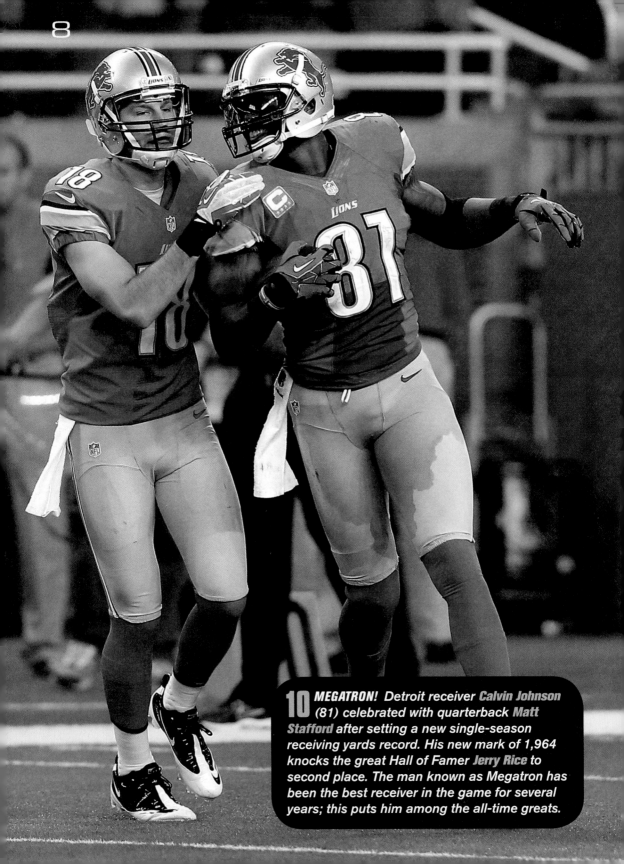

10 ***MEGATRON!*** *Detroit receiver* *Calvin Johnson* *(81) celebrated with quarterback* *Matt* *Stafford* *after setting a new single-season receiving yards record. His new mark of 1,964 knocks the great Hall of Famer* *Jerry Rice* *to second place. The man known as Megatron has been the best receiver in the game for several years; this puts him among the all-time greats.*

9 **MIGUEL MIGUEL MIGUEL!** *A hitter who combines power with a solid average is very rare. A hitter who can also knock in runs left and right is rarer still. In 2012, Detroit Tigers third baseman Miguel Cabrera did all three of those things better than anyone else in the American League. By leading the AL in homers, average, and RBI, he became the first player since Boston legend Carl Yastrzemski to win the coveted Triple Crown (plus the AL MVP award!).*

8 **BOSTON STRONG!** *Just as the 2013 Boston Marathon was ending on April 15, a pair of bombs exploded near the finish line. A day of joy suddenly became one of terror. Three people were killed and more than 250 people were injured. Police quickly tracked down the bombers. The attack inspired people to support Boston. Red Sox players wore "Boston Strong" patches.* **David Ortiz** *gave a rousing speech at a game that honored victims and first responders. Boston strong!*

7 BYE, BYE BECKHAM *After helping the L.A. Galaxy win its second straight MLS title, soccer superstar David Beckham left for a short stint with a team in France. After that was over (and he won another league championship), he announced his retirement from the sport. In 20 years, Beckham had become one of the most famous athletes on the planet and helped his teams win title after title.*

6

GREAT SCOT! *The tennis championships at Wimbledon near London is one of the world's most famous sporting events. But no one from Great Britain had won since 1937.* ***Andy Murray,*** *from Scotland, a part of Great Britain, changed that in July 2013. He crushed Novak Djokovic to win the fabled tournament and its golden trophy, and thrill millions of his fans.*

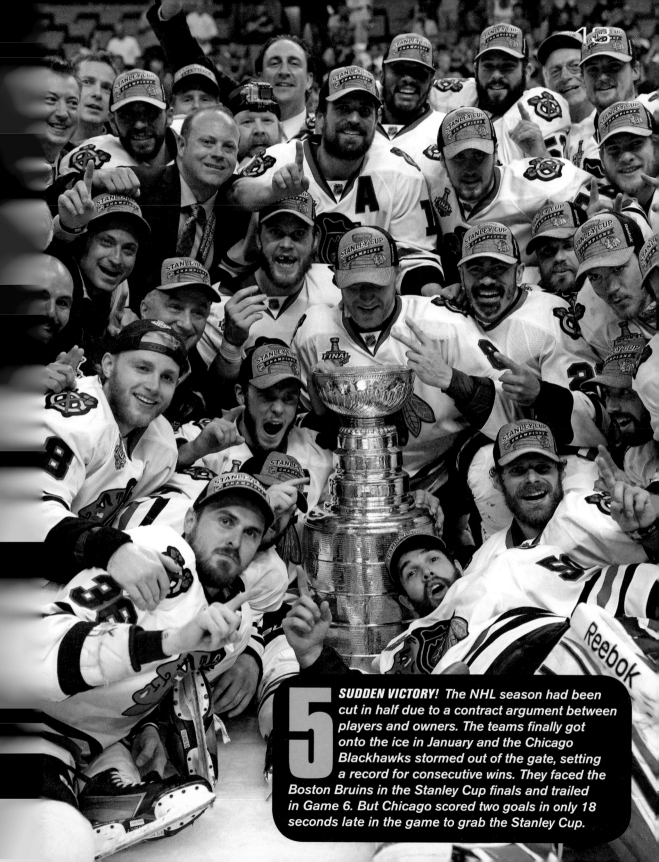

5 **SUDDEN VICTORY!** The NHL season had been cut in half due to a contract argument between players and owners. The teams finally got onto the ice in January and the Chicago Blackhawks stormed out of the gate, setting a record for consecutive wins. They faced the Boston Bruins in the Stanley Cup finals and trailed in Game 6. But Chicago scored two goals in only 18 seconds late in the game to grab the Stanley Cup.

4

A GIANT WIN! *Though most experts did not pick them at the start of the year, by the end of the baseball season, the San Francisco Giants were the best. Led by a super pitching staff, the Giants swept the Detroit Tigers to win the franchise's ninth World Series title.*

3

MIAMI MAGIC!
Led by all-world superstar LeBron James (with ball; he scored 37 points in Game 7!), the Miami Heat repeated as NBA champs in 2013. Miami dominated in the regular season, but in the NBA Finals, the always-tough San Antonio Spurs made the Heat really work for the title. A last-second shot saved the Heat in Game 6, and James's heroics cleared the way in Game 7.

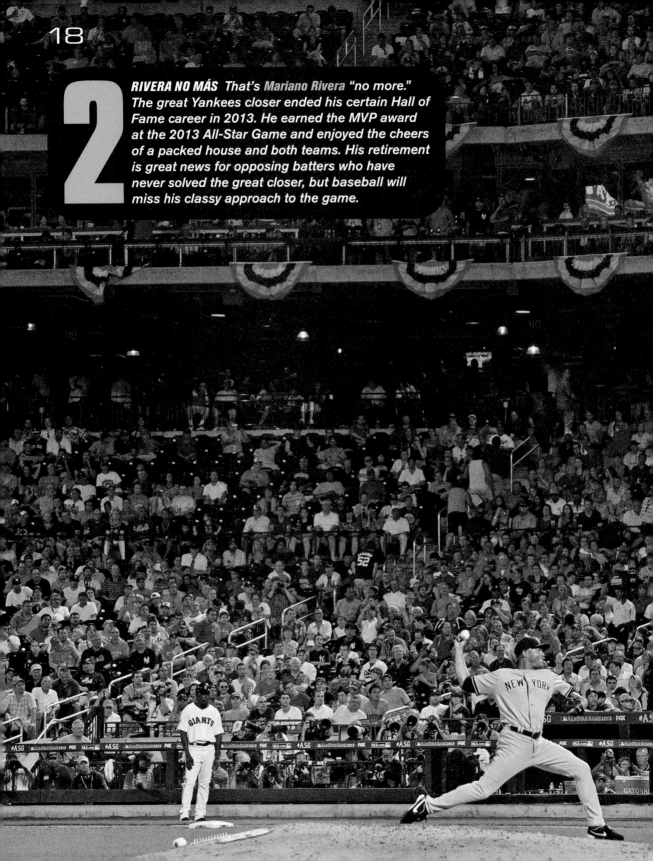

2

RIVERA NO MÁS *That's Mariano Rivera "no more." The great Yankees closer ended his certain Hall of Fame career in 2013. He earned the MVP award at the 2013 All-Star Game and enjoyed the cheers of a packed house and both teams. His retirement is great news for opposing batters who have never solved the great closer, but baseball will miss his classy approach to the game.*

1

SUPER SUPER BOWL! *No matter what team you root for, you want the Super Bowl to be packed with great plays and come down to the final seconds. Well, Super Bowl XLVII had all that and more. Fans saw long touchdown passes, a record kickoff return, and even a stadium blackout that forced a long timeout! At the end, the Baltimore Ravens held the San Francisco 49ers out of the end zone on a final drive and hung on to win 34–31 and earn their second Lombardi Trophy.*

JACOBY'S JAUNT!
Jacoby Jones of the Baltimore Ravens heads to the end zone in the Super Bowl. His record-setting kickoff return helped the Ravens cement their second NFL title with a dramatic 34–31 win over the San Francisco 49ers.

NFL

Rookies and Ravens!

S ome of the most memorable players of the 2012 NFL season were its youngest. With standout performances from several first-year players, 2012 will go down as the "Year of the Rookie QB."

First-overall pick **Andrew Luck** was handed the Colts starting job and made the most of it. He set a rookie record for passing yards and led Indianapolis to the playoffs. Washington's **Robert Griffin III** was the second-overall choice, and he also led his team to the playoffs. "RG3" set a rookie record for passer rating. The third superstar young passer, **Russell Wilson** of Seattle, had a rough first half of the season. He made up for it in the second half, guiding Seattle to a playoff spot and tying a rookie-season record for TD passes. Finally, second-year passer **Colin Kaepernick**, though not a rookie, had his first starts in the pros and led the 49ers to the Super Bowl.

Young QBs were not the only big story, of course. A veteran passer gave fans some of the best memories of the season. **Peyton Manning** had missed the entire 2011 season with a neck injury. The longtime Colts QB had been let go by Indianapolis. Many experts thought his Hall of Fame career was over. Manning had other ideas, however, and signed with Denver. After some early struggles, he led the Broncos to one of the league's best records. They finished the season with 11 straight wins. Though his team lost to the Ravens in a playoff classic, Manning was named the Comeback Player of the Year.

That Ravens-Broncos playoff game was one of many great postseason stories. Several games featured exciting comebacks. Others featured rising stars putting up big numbers. For a complete report on the postseason games, see page 26.

The regular season had many highlights, too, including some of the highest-scoring games of all time. A couple of surprise teams had two of the best records in the league. The Houston Texans rambled to an 11−1 mark before hitting some bumps to finish at 12−4. The Atlanta Falcons had the best record in the NFC and nearly made the big dance in the end. The season also saw big NFL records fall. Detroit wide receiver **Calvin Johnson** got the biggest one (see page 31), while Minnesota running back **Adrian Peterson** nearly got another.

The veteran Manning showed the kids how it is done.

2,097

That's Adrian Peterson's rushing yardage total, the second-highest in NFL history. Peterson missed setting a new record by only nine yards!

And kicker **David Akers** tied an all-time best with a little help. See page 32 for four quarters of regular-season highlights.

After all the dust settled from a wild regular season and an exciting playoff run, the Baltimore Ravens faced the San Francisco 49ers in Super Bowl XLVII. Kaepernick continued his great season by almost leading the Niners to victory. He ran for one score and threw for another. However, he didn't have enough magic to stop MVP **Joe Flacco** and the Ravens, who won 34–31.

The game did feature the first-ever Super Bowl blackout! Just after the second half started, most of the lights in the Louisiana Superdome went out! More than 30 minutes later, the game resumed. A stadium electrical relay had caused the problem. The full Super Bowl story is on page 28.

2012 Final Regular-Season Standings

AFC EAST	W	L	T
New England Patriots	12	4	
Miami Dolphins	7	9	
New York Jets	6	10	
Buffalo Bills	6	10	

AFC NORTH	W	L	T
Baltimore Ravens	10	6	
Cincinnati Bengals	10	6	
Pittsburgh Steelers	8	8	
Cleveland Browns	5	11	

AFC SOUTH	W	L	T
Houston Texans	12	4	
Indianapolis Colts	11	5	
Tennessee Titans	6	10	
Jacksonville Jaguars	2	14	

AFC WEST	W	L	T
Denver Broncos	13	3	
San Diego Chargers	7	9	
Oakland Raiders	4	12	
Kansas City Chiefs	2	14	

NFC EAST	W	L	T
Washington Redskins	10	6	
New York Giants	9	7	
Dallas Cowboys	8	8	
Philadelphia Eagles	4	12	

NFC NORTH	W	L	T
Green Bay Packers	11	5	
Minnesota Vikings	10	6	
Chicago Bears	10	6	
Detroit Lions	4	12	

NFC SOUTH	W	L	T
Atlanta Falcons	13	3	
Carolina Panthers	7	9	
New Orleans Saints	7	9	
Tampa Bay Buccaneers	7	9	

NFC WEST	W	L	T
San Francisco 49ers	11	4	1
Seattle Seahawks	11	5	
St. Louis Rams	7	8	1
Arizona Cardinals	5	11	

2012 Playoffs

Wild-Card Playoffs

Texans 19–Bengals 10

Houston's **Arian Foster** had his third straight 100-yard playoff game and scored a key touchdown. The only Bengals score came on an interception return.

Ravens 24–Colts 9

Andrew Luck's magic rookie season came to an end, while legendary Ravens linebacker **Ray Lewis** got another game. Baltimore's **Anquan Boldin** had a key touchdown catch and the Ravens defense pounded the Colts.

Packers 24–Vikings 10

The Vikings' chances ended when starting QB **Christian Ponder** couldn't play. Backup **Joe Webb** had not thrown an NFL pass, and even the great **Adrian Peterson** was not enough by himself.

Seahawks 24–Redskins 14

The battle of rookie QBs went to Seattle's **Russell Wilson**. Wilson got a lot of help from running back **Marshawn Lynch**, who had 132 yards and a TD. Washington's **Robert Griffin III** was playing on an injured knee, and it got worse when he fell late in the game.

Divisional Playoffs

Patriots 41–Texans 28

Tom Brady won his 17th postseason game, setting a new NFL record. He led the Patriots to the AFC title game with three touchdowns and 344 yards passing. Running back **Shane Vereen** was a surprise star, scoring three times after doing so only four times in two seasons!

Wilson led the Seahawks to the second round.

Gore stepped in for two playoff scores.

49ers 45–Packers 31

Colin Kaepernick had the greatest running day by a QB in NFL history! The multitalented young player ran for 181 yards, including a 56-yard score, to lead the 49ers to victory. He also had two scoring passes. Not bad for a player making just his eighth start in the NFL!

Conference Championships

49ers 28–Falcons 24

Kaepernick used his arm to send the 49ers to the Super Bowl. After the 49ers fell behind 17–0, Kaepernick led them to four touchdowns. He threw for 233 yards and a score, while running back **Frank Gore** had a big game with a pair of TDs. The 49ers defense shut down the Falcons to end the game.

Ravens 28–Patriots 13

Ray Lewis's last game would be the Super Bowl after he and the Ravens beat **Tom Brady** and the Patriots. Down 13–7 at halftime, Baltimore dominated the second half, scoring three times. It was the first time that the Brady-led Patriots had ever lost a game at home after leading at halftime. The Ravens' surge was led by **Anquan Boldin**, who made two TD catches. Meanwhile, the Ravens D kept Brady and the Pats offense quiet.

Ravens 38–Broncos 35

Joe Flacco threw a stunning last-minute 70-yard TD pass to tie the game. Baltimore won in the second quarter of overtime after **Justin Tucker** kicked a field goal. Even though **Trindon Holliday** set a record by returning a kickoff and a punt for TDs, Denver's **Peyton Manning** could not end his dream comeback season with a victory.

Falcons 30–Seahawks 28

Down 20–0 early, Seattle rallied to take the lead late in the fourth quarter. However, they left **Matt Ryan** and the Falcons enough time for a game-winning drive. Ryan coolly led his team into field-goal range, and then **Matt Bryant** hit a 49-yard kick for the big win.

SUPER BOWL XLVII • NEW ORLEANS

Return of the Ravens!

NFL fans enjoyed another thrilling Super Bowl when the 49ers met the Ravens at the Superdome in New Orleans. As with most recent NFL title games, this one was not decided until the final seconds.

The game also saw an important first. Two brothers—**John** and **Jim Harbaugh**—were the head coaches of the opposing teams!

The Ravens dominated the first half, bottling up 49ers QB **Colin Kaepernick**. They picked off one of his passes (the first one ever thrown by a Niners QB in a Super Bowl!) and recovered a fumble. Ravens QB

Joe Flacco threw three TD passes in the half, including a 56-yard bomb to **Jacoby Jones**. After Jones fell to make the catch, he scrambled up and dodged two tacklers for the score. That made it 21–6 Baltimore, and the Niners hoped that halftime would help them regroup.

It didn't.

The first play of the second half was the longest in Super Bowl history. Baltimore's Jacoby Jones returned the kickoff 108 yards and the Niners trailed by 22 points.

Just a few moments later, however, most of the lights in the Superdome went out! Fans at home watched a silent screen for

Ray Lewis (#52) wrapped up his Hall of Fame career by wrapping up Niners!

SUPER JOE!

He's not the flashiest or the most famous quarterback in a pass-happy NFL, but **Joe Flacco** is one thing for sure: the current Super Bowl champion. Flacco threw for 287 yards and three TD passes and was named the game's MVP. He tied **Joe Montana** by throwing 11 TDs and zero interceptions in one postseason. In the offseason, Flacco signed a contract making him one of the NFL's highest-paid players.

several moments. Fans in the dark stands did the wave and watched cheerleaders. Players and coaches just stretched and waited. Thirty-four minutes later, the lights were finally back on and play resumed.

The hot Ravens cooled off, and the Niners heated up with the lights. San Francisco scored 25 points the rest of the way, while holding Baltimore to just six.

The comeback was not enough, however. The 49ers were down by five with just under two minutes to play. They reached the Ravens' seven-yard line and had four shots at the end zone. All four fell short and Baltimore held on to win the game.

It was the Ravens' second

Super Bowl title; they also won XXXV. It was future Hall of Fame linebacker **Ray Lewis**'s last game, too. "There's no better way to go out," he said, "than to win a championship with teammates like these."

SUPER BOWL XLVII

TEAM	1Q	2Q	3Q	4Q	FINAL
Baltimore	**7**	**14**	**7**	**6**	**34**
San Francisco	**3**	**3**	**17**	**8**	**31**

SCORING

1Q: BAL	A. Boldin, 13 yards from J. Flacco (Tucker kick)
1Q: SF	D. Akers, 36-yard FG
2Q: BAL	D. Pitta, 1 yard from J. Flacco (Tucker kick)
2Q: BAL	J. Jones, 56 yards from J. Flacco (Tucker kick)
2Q: SF	D. Akers, 27-yard FG
3Q: BAL	J. Jones, 108-yard KO return (Tucker kick)
3Q: SF	M. Crabtree, 31 yards from C. Kaepernick (Akers kick)
3Q: SF	F. Gore, 6-yard run (Akers kick)
3Q: SF	D. Akers, 34-yards FG
4Q: BAL	J. Tucker, 19-yard FG
4Q: SF	C. Kaepernick, 15-yard run
4Q: BAL	J. Tucker, 38-yard FG
4Q: SF	Safety, Koch runs out of end zone

The Leaders

2,097 RUSHING YARDS
Adrian Peterson, Vikings

15 RUSHING TDS
Arian Foster, Texans

5,177 PASSING YARDS
43 TOUCHDOWN PASSES
Drew Brees, Saints

1,964 RECEIVING YARDS
122 RECEPTIONS
◀◀◀**Calvin Johnson**, Lions

153 POINTS
Stephen Gostkowski, Patriots

35 FIELD GOALS
Blair Walsh, Vikings

164 TACKLES
Luke Kuechly, Panthers

20.5 SACKS
J. J. Watt, Texans

9 INTERCEPTIONS
Tim Jennings, Bears

AWARD WINNERS

NFL MVP
ADRIAN PETERSON
RB, VIKINGS

OFFENSIVE PLAYER OF THE YEAR
ADRIAN PETERSON
RB, VIKINGS

DEFENSIVE PLAYER OF THE YEAR
J. J. WATT
DE, TEXANS

OFFENSIVE ROOKIE OF THE YEAR
ROBERT GRIFFIN III
QB, REDSKINS

DEFENSIVE ROOKIE OF THE YEAR
LUKE KUECHLY
LB, PANTHERS

COMEBACK PLAYER OF THE YEAR
PEYTON MANNING
QB, BRONCOS

COACH OF THE YEAR
BRUCE ARIANS
COLTS

WALTER PAYTON AWARD
(Given for community service)
JASON WITTEN
TE, COWBOYS

MEGATRON!

Detroit's **Calvin Johnson** had one of the greatest seasons ever put together by a wide receiver. He set a new single-season record with 1,964 receiving yards, passing the great **Jerry Rice**. Johnson's 122 catches tied for third-most all-time. He did all that while being unable to practice for most of November due to knee and ankle injuries. But he suited up for every game, and though every defense aimed to stop him, the man they call "Megatron" transformed the NFL record book.

108.0

For the second year in a row, **Aaron Rodgers** of the Packers led the NFL in passer rating. He's also the all-time career leader. Passer rating combines several QB stat categories so that one number can be used to compare all the league's passers.

Stevan Ridley scored one of the Patriots' six TDs in Week 4.

55-yard field goal to tie the game, then a 38-yarder in overtime to win.

✱ Peyton Power: Peyton Manning threw his 400th career TD in a Week 1 win over Pittsburgh.

✱ Flying Cardinals: Arizona continued its hot start, upsetting the Patriots in Week 2. They moved to 4-0 with a Week 4 overtime win over Miami.

✱ Long Distance: In Week 1, San Francisco kicker **David Akers** tied an NFL record with a 63-yard field goal. He got some help when it hit the crossbar and bounced over!

✱ Bumpy Beginning: Indy's **Andrew Luck** had a rough start to his NFL career. He threw three interceptions as the Colts got stomped by the Bears.

✱ Two for One: A pair of great stories from the Vikings' Week 1 win: **Adrian Peterson** amazed fans by returning from a serious knee injury. Rookie kicker **Blair Walsh** hit a

✱ Don't Leave!: In Week 3, fans had to stay all the way to the end. Seven games were decided on the final play or in the final minute.

✱ Pour It On: In Week 4, New England trailed Buffalo 14-7 at the half. Then the Pats went wild, scoring six straight TDs in the second half to win, 52-28!

✱ Sad Saints: Hit by suspensions of their head coach and key defenders, the Saints hit the brakes. New Orleans lost its first four games.

Second Quarter
NFL WEEKS 5–8

* **New Record:** In Week 5, **Drew Brees** of the Saints broke one of the oldest NFL records. With a TD pass in his 48th straight game, he topped the great **Johnny Unitas**'s record of 47. "Johnny U" had been the best since 1960!

* **An Emotional Day:** Also in Week 5, Indianapolis faced a new challenge. Head coach **Chuck Pagano** had to miss the game as he began treatment for cancer. Inspired, **Andrew Luck** and the Colts rallied to upset the Packers.

* **Wonderful Wilson:** In Week 6, Seattle's rookie sensation **Russell Wilson** put on a show. He rallied the Seahawks to two touchdowns late in the fourth quarter. The final 46-yard strike to **Sidney Rice** made Seattle an upset winner over New England.

* **Comeback King:** The great **Peyton Manning** has led his teams to many amazing wins. But he had never done what he did on Monday night in Week 6. Trailing 24–0 at the half, Denver put on an amazing second-half display and rallied to beat San Diego, 35–24. It was one of the biggest comebacks in NFL history, and tied for the best comeback in a road game.

* **First-Half Favorites:** As the season's first half ended, the Falcons, Texans, and Bears had only two losses among them.

Brees broke a record some thought could never be topped!

Third Quarter

✱ Wow: Doug Martin of the Buccaneers got the second half of the season off to a blazing start. The rookie running back ran for 251 yards and four touchdowns against the Raiders. Three of his TD runs went for 45 yards or longer—the first time a player has ever done that in one game.

✱ Overtime Thriller: When the Texans played the Jaguars in Week 11, Houston QB **Matt Schaub** threw for 527 yards, tied for second-most in NFL history. Receiver **Andre Johnson** had 48 of those yards on a catch-and-run for the winning score in overtime. Jacksonville rookie **Justin Blackmon** had 236 receiving yards, the third-most by a rookie in a single game.

✱ Stunning Second Quarter: The Jets would like to forget the second quarter of their Week 12 loss to the Patriots. New England scored 35 points while having the ball for just over two minutes. No surprise: They won 49–19.

✱ No Winners: In Week 10, the Rams and 49ers played to the first tie in the NFL since 2008, as each team missed possible game-winning field goals. The final was 24–24.

✱ Splish, Splash: In the third quarter of Miami's comeback win over Seattle in Week 12, there was a brief interruption. The field sprinklers suddenly went off, spritzing players and coaches for several minutes!

✱ Ray Saves the Day: With 1:37 left in the game and down by three points, Baltimore needed a miracle. **Ray Rice** delivered. He took a short pass and changed 4th-and-29 into a first down. The Ravens tied the game shortly after and won in overtime. In January, Rice's rumble was named the NFL's Play of the Year.

Rice saved the day for the Ravens.

Fourth Quarter
NFL WEEKS 13-17

✱ Streak Over: Remember **Drew Brees**'s new record for games with a TD pass? It ended in Week 13. Atlanta picked him off five times and kept him out of the end zone in a 23–13 win.

✱ A Lot of Luck: The Colts' **Andrew Luck** led the Colts to the winning touchdown on the final play against Detroit in Week 13. He gambled by throwing to **Donnie Avery** at about the five-yard line. If Avery had been tackled, the game would have ended with the Lions on top. But Luck saw that the path was clear to the end zone and made the throw.

✱ Got Your Back: Robert Griffin III was not the only rookie QB to star for Washington. After he was hurt against Baltimore in Week 13, fellow first-year passer **Kirk Cousins** came off the bench to help Washington get a win.

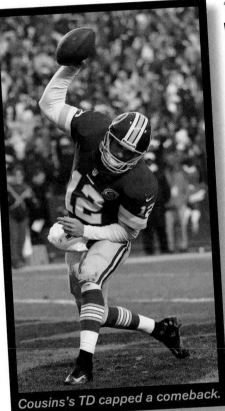

Cousins's TD capped a comeback.

✱ Points Parade: In Weeks 14, 15, and 16, Seattle put together a streak for the record books. They started their scoring binge with a 58–0 win over Arizona. They beat Buffalo 50–17 the following week. The wins marked the first time an NFL team had scored 50 points in back-to-back games since 1950! They wrapped up a three-game scoring attack with a 42–13 win over the 49ers.

✱ Comeback: After completing treatment for cancer, Colts coach **Chuck Pagano** returned to the sidelines in Week 17. His team treated him to a 28–16 win over Houston.

✱ Just Short: On his final run of 2012, Minnesota's **Adrian Peterson** set his team up for a game-winning field goal that put them in the playoffs. He fell nine yards short of the NFL single-season record, but it was worth it!

ROOKIE QB REPORT CARD

The 2012 season was the year of the rookie QB. Led by the five rookies graded here, first-year passers had a bigger impact than in any other NFL season. They combined for 15 300-yard passing games, breaking the old record by 8 games. Seven different rookie passers led their teams to a win. The previous high was five. Here's a rundown on how they did individually:

◄◄◄ ANDREW LUCK, COLTS

A Set new rookie record with 4,374 passing yards and led Colts to a 8-win improvement over 2011.

RUSSELL WILSON, SEAHAWKS

A Led Seattle to playoff win while tying rookie record with 26 TD passes.

ROBERT GRIFFIN III, REDSKINS

A- Energized struggling team and led them to playoffs. Future clouded by knee injury, but has potential to become dynamic leader. Set rookie record with 102.4 passer rating.

RYAN TANNEHILL, DOLPHINS

C- Team only scored 30-plus points twice, so this rookie had to show good leadership.

BRANDON WEEDEN, BROWNS

D Lost first five games of the season, but later led upset of Steelers. Leading a young team, has a long way to go.

46

That's how many games rookie QBs won in 2012. The old record was only 23.

Blair Walsh was King of the Kickers!

Fantasy Stars

Fantasy football continues to grow, with millions of people now playing the game online with friends. It's a great way to get closer to the sport by choosing your favorite players and going head-to-head with friends. Here are the top-scoring fantasy football players by position from 2012, according to the NFL.com scoring system.

QB: DREW BREES, 345 points

RB: ADRIAN PETERSON, 307

WR: CALVIN JOHNSON, 220

TE: JIMMY GRAHAM, 152

K: BLAIR WALSH, 161

DEF: BEARS, 222

MORE
RECORD BREAKERS

Here's a look at some other record-breaking performances from 2012:

✸ **Pick Six!** NFL defenders set a new single-season record by returning 66 interceptions for touchdowns. **Charles Tillman** of the Bears and **Janoris Jenkins** of the Rams had three each.

✸ **Close Games!** The NFL played 22 overtime games in 2012. That tied the all-time single-season high. Also, 128 games were decided by eight points or less. That's the most ever in one season!

✸ **High Scoring!** NFL teams scored 11,651 points in 2012, breaking a record set in 2011!

✸ **Good Average!** Kansas City's **Jamaal Charles** now has a 5.8-yards-per-carry average. That makes him the new all-time leader among running backs.

✸ **Long Distance!** Minnesota rookie kicker **Blair Walsh** had 10 field goals of 50 yards or more, the most ever for a single season.

✸ **Sore Arm!** Detroit QB **Matthew Stafford** attempted 727 passes in 2012, more than any other QB in a single season.

Hall of Fame Class of 2013

Welcome to these new members of football's most famous club:

LARRY ALLEN
T, Cowboys, 49ers

11-time Pro Bowl player, outstanding run blocker, named to NFL All-Decade Teams for 1990s and 2000s.

CRIS CARTER ▶▶▶
WR, Vikings, Dolphins

When he retired in 2001, Carter was second all-time in receptions, receiving yards, and touchdown catches.

CURLEY CULP
DE, Chiefs, Oilers

Tall and powerful pass-rusher helped Chiefs win Super Bowl IV, was 1975 Defensive Player of the Year with Oilers.

JONATHAN OGDEN
T, Ravens

11-time Pro Bowl player, helped Ravens win Super Bowl XXXV, helped Jamal Lewis reach 2,000 yards in 2003

BILL PARCELLS
Coach, Giants, Jets, Patriots, Cowboys

Won two Super Bowls with Giants, turned

280

That's the number of people who are members of the Pro Football Hall of Fame, which opened in 1963 in Canton, Ohio.

Jets and Patriots from losing teams into playoff teams, known as "The Big Tuna."

DAVE ROBINSON
LB, Packers, Redskins

Named to All-Decade Team for 1960s, was part of defense that won Super Bowls I and II under coach Vince Lombardi.

WARREN SAPP
DT, Buccaneers, Raiders

1999 Defensive Player of the Year, racked up 96.5 sacks, named to seven Pro Bowls, helped Tampa Bay win Super Bowl XXXVII.

NFL DRAFT TOP TEN

Linemen on both sides of the ball were the most popular picks.

PICK	PLAYER/SCHOOL	NFL TEAM
1	**Eric Fisher**, T	Kansas City ▶▶▶
2	**Luke Joeckel**, T	Jacksonville
3	**Dion Jordan**, DE	Miami
4	**Lane Johnson**, T	Philadelphia
5	**Ziggy Ansah**, DE	Detroit
6	**Barkevious Mingo**, DE	Cleveland
7	**Jonathan Cooper**, G	Arizona
8	**Tavon Austin**, WR	St. Louis
9	**Dee Milliner**, CB	N. Y. Jets
10	**Chance Warmack**, T	Tennessee

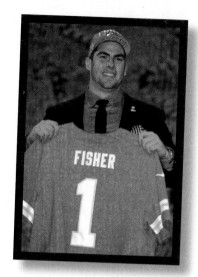

JOLLY GOOD NFL SHOW!

Most people in Great Britain think "football" is a game the U.S. calls soccer. But the NFL brand of football is becoming popular "across the pond." The NFL says 11 million people in the U.K. are NFL fans. They must be right, because both of the 2013 games in London sold out in January! The teams will play at famous Wembley Stadium, where the Patriots beat the Rams, 45–7, in 2012. Plus, the Jaguars are also set to return from 2014–2016 as well. English fans are just learning the game, but the NFL is ready to put on a show!

2013 LONDON NFL GAMES
Sept. 29: Pittsburgh vs. Minnesota
Oct. 27: Jacksonville vs. San Francisco

COACHING-GO-ROUND

Eight NFL teams have new head coaches for 2013.

COACH	NEW TEAM	OLD JOB
Bruce Arians	Cardinals	Colts
Gus Bradley	Jaguars	Seahawks
Rob Chudzinski	Browns	Panthers
Chip Kelly	Eagles	Univ. of Oregon
Doug Marrone	Bills	Syracuse Univ.
Mike McCoy	Chargers	Broncos
Andy Reid	Chiefs	Eagles
Marc Trestman	Bears	Alouettes

For the Record

Super Bowl Winners

GAME	SEASON	WINNING TEAM	LOSING TEAM	SCORE	SITE
XLVII	2012	**Baltimore**	San Francisco	**34–31**	New Orleans
XLVI	2011	**N.Y. Giants**	New England	**21–17**	Indianapolis
XLV	2010	**Green Bay**	Pittsburgh	**31–25**	Dallas
XLIV	2009	**New Orleans**	Indianapolis	**31–17**	South Florida
XLIII	2008	**Pittsburgh**	Arizona	**27–23**	Tampa
XLII	2007	**N.Y. Giants**	New England	**17–14**	Glendale, Ariz.
XLI	2006	**Indianapolis**	Chicago	**29–17**	South Florida
XL	2005	**Pittsburgh**	Seattle	**21–10**	Detroit
XXXIX	2004	**New England**	Philadelphia	**24–21**	Jacksonville
XXXVIII	2003	**New England**	Carolina	**32–29**	Houston
XXXVII	2002	**Tampa Bay**	Oakland	**48–21**	San Diego
XXXVI	2001	**New England**	St. Louis	**20–17**	New Orleans
XXXV	2000	**Baltimore**	N.Y. Giants	**34–7**	Tampa
XXXIV	1999	**St. Louis**	Tennessee	**23–16**	Atlanta
XXXIII	1998	**Denver**	Atlanta	**34–19**	South Florida
XXXII	1997	**Denver**	Green Bay	**31–24**	San Diego
XXXI	1996	**Green Bay**	New England	**35–21**	New Orleans
XXX	1995	**Dallas**	Pittsburgh	**27–17**	Tempe, Ariz.
XXIX	1994	**San Francisco**	San Diego	**49–26**	South Florida
XXVIII	1993	**Dallas**	Buffalo	**30–13**	Atlanta
XXVII	1992	**Dallas**	Buffalo	**52–17**	Pasadena

GAME	SEASON	WINNING TEAM	LOSING TEAM	SCORE	SITE
XXVI	1991	Washington	Buffalo	37–24	Minneapolis
XXV	1990	N.Y. Giants	Buffalo	20–19	Tampa
XXIV	1989	San Francisco	Denver	55–10	New Orleans
XXIII	1988	San Francisco	Cincinnati	20–16	South Florida
XXII	1987	Washington	Denver	42–10	San Diego
XXI	1986	N.Y. Giants	Denver	39–20	Pasadena
XX	1985	Chicago	New England	46–10	New Orleans
XIX	1984	San Francisco	Miami	38–16	Stanford
XVIII	1983	L.A. Raiders	Washington	38–9	Tampa
XVII	1982	Washington	Miami	27–17	Pasadena
XVI	1981	San Francisco	Cincinnati	26–21	Pontiac, Mich.
XV	1980	Oakland	Philadelphia	27–10	New Orleans
XIV	1979	Pittsburgh	Los Angeles	31–19	Pasadena
XIII	1978	Pittsburgh	Dallas	35–31	Miami
XII	1977	Dallas	Denver	27–10	New Orleans
XI	1976	Oakland	Minnesota	32–14	Pasadena
X	1975	Pittsburgh	Dallas	21–17	Miami
IX	1974	Pittsburgh	Minnesota	16–6	New Orleans
VIII	1973	Miami	Minnesota	24–7	Houston
VII	1972	Miami	Washington	14–7	Los Angeles
VI	1971	Dallas	Miami	24–3	New Orleans
V	1970	Baltimore	Dallas	16–13	Miami
IV	1969	Kansas City	Minnesota	23–7	New Orleans
III	1968	N.Y. Jets	Baltimore	16–7	Miami
II	1967	Green Bay	Oakland	33–14	Miami
I	1966	Green Bay	Kansas City	35–10	Los Angeles

COLLEGE FOOTBALL

THERE THEY GO AGAIN!
For the first time since 2004, college football had a repeat national champion. Alabama defeated Notre Dame in the BCS Championship Game to capture its second title in a row and its third in four years.

Alabama ...Again!

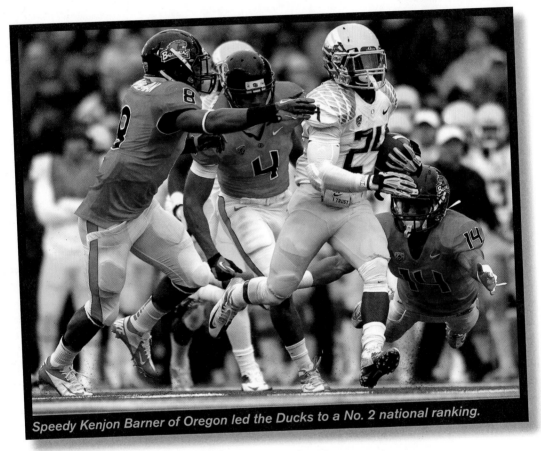

Speedy Kenjon Barner of Oregon led the Ducks to a No. 2 national ranking.

College football kicked off in August 2012 and kept playing until early January. After all the touchdowns, the big plays, the amazing catches, and the crunching tackles, 2012 ended up like 2011: Alabama repeated as the national champion. The Crimson Tide were the first team since USC (2003–2004) to claim a share of back-to-back titles. It was also Alabama's third championship in four years.

Notre Dame, Alabama's opponent in the BCS Championship Game (see page 46) enjoyed a return to football glory. Few schools have as much college football greatness in their history as N.D. Their run to the BCS game thrilled millions of their loyal fans. They escaped two overtime thrillers—over Stanford and Pittsburgh—while achieving the only undefeated record in the country in the regular season.

Many other teams, however, gave those two a run for their money.

On October 7, three teams, No. 3 Florida, No. 4 LSU, and No. 5 Georgia,

FINAL 2012 AP TOP 10

1.	**Alabama**	13-1
2.	**Oregon**	12-1
3.	**Ohio State**	12-0
4.	**Notre Dame**	12-1
5.	**Georgia**	12-2
6.	**Texas A&M**	11-2
7.	**Stanford**	12-2
8.	**South Carolina**	11-2
9.	**Florida**	11-2
10.	**Florida State**	12-2

fans and opponents.

Other teams tried to climb the mountain only to fall back. Kansas State reached No. 1 for the first time ever. Quarterback Collin Klein dazzled with his 23 touchdown runs of the season. Once they were on top, however, K-State stumbled, losing to Baylor. They lost on the same weekend No. 2 Oregon fell. That was the first time in BCS history that the top two teams lost on the same day.

Florida made a move, too. But after reaching the No. 2 spot, they lost to SEC rival Georgia. West Virginia was the hot team early on. Super QB Geno Smith lit up scoreboards as the Mountaineers got off to a 5–0 start. But a loss to Texas Tech was the first of several more defeats.

who had a shot at the top spot all lost their games.

USC came into the season expecting great things. With the great Matt Barkley at quarterback and a host of talented offensive players, the Trojans had national-title hopes. A loss to Stanford on September 15 ended that dream early. USC wound up with an unexpected 7–6 record. Stanford, on the other hand, showed that it could remain a national power even without Andrew Luck, who had moved to the NFL. The Cardinal not only upset USC, they handed Oregon its only loss of the season. Had the Ducks not lost that game, Oregon would have played for the national title. As it was, their high-flying offense continued to amaze

Hard-running QB Collin Klein of Kansas State

Even Alabama lost a game, falling 29–24 to Texas A&M. The Aggies had one of the great stories of the college football season in their quarterback, Johnny Manziel. Only a freshman, he put on an all-around offensive display that helped him earn the Heisman Trophy (see page 53). Alabama, however, bounced back from that loss.

A big comeback win over SEC rival LSU sent them into the SEC Championship Game. Since the last six BCS champs came from the SEC, the winner of that game figured to make it seven straight. By knocking off a tough Georgia team, Alabama put itself in position to do just that.

With three national titles in four years, Alabama has made itself the latest college football dynasty.

2011 BCS Championship
Roll, Tide!

Alabama's Ha'Sean Clinton-Dix makes a pickoff.

The final score was 42–14, but it wasn't that close. Alabama won its third BCS Championship in four years by absolutely dominating Notre Dame. The Crimson Tide offense was clicking, showing off its many talents. On defense, they nearly repeated their shutout performance in the previous BCS game.

On the opening drive, Alabama moved 82 yards for a touchdown run by **Eddie Lacy**. The big running back was named the game's offensive MVP after running for 140 yards and that big opening score. A Notre Dame defense that had allowed an average of only 10 points per game gave up 21 points in this game's first 20 minutes.

Quarterback **A. J. McCarron** was nearly perfect. He completed 20 of 28 attempts for 264 yards and four touchdowns. **Amari Cooper** caught two of those TD passes.

Alabama rolled out to a 28–0 halftime lead, depressing the thousands of Irish fans in the stands at the Orange Bowl in Miami. Notre Dame managed to score a few, but that didn't help with the final score.

For Notre Dame, it was disappointing. The school with eight national titles— second-most all-time—fell short of No. 9.

For coach **Nick Saban** and Alabama, however, it was time to celebrate. Going for three in a row will be even tougher. No school has ever done that . . . yet.

Sugar Bowl
Louisville 33–Florida 23
The Cardinals pulled one of the biggest upsets of bowl season by knocking off No. 3 Florida. A pick-six late in the game clinched the big win.

Rose Bowl
Stanford 20–Wisconsin 14
It was a sea of red in Pasadena, but Stanford bottled up Wisconsin's running game. The Cardinal won their first Rose Bowl since 1972.

Fiesta Bowl
Oregon 35–Kansas State 17
The Wildcats didn't know what hit them as the Ducks rolled to an easy win.

Orange Bowl
Florida State 31–
Northern Illinois 10
Northern Illinois crashed the BCS party after a terrific 12–1 season. They hit the wall, however, as FSU enjoyed a home-state advantage.

15

Alabama has won more national football championships than any other school.

2012	1964
2011	1961
2009	1941*
1992	1934*
1979	1930
1978	1926
1973*	1925
1965*	(*co-champion)

CRIMSON TIDE

Other Bowl Highlights

GATOR BOWL
Northwestern has been playing football since 1882. They've been to 10 bowl games in the last half-century . . . but they lost all of them. That streak ended in December. The Wildcats beat Mississippi State, 34–20. It was Northwestern's first bowl game victory since 1949!

NEW MEXICO BOWL
Arizona had the wildest comeback of the bowl season. They trailed Nevada by 13 points with less than a minute to go. They scored, however, and then recovered the onside kick. Three passes later, it was 49–48 Arizona . . . game over!

POINSETTIA BOWL
BYU's **Kyle Van Noy** seemed like he was a one-man team. Against San Diego State, the linebacker made eight tackles, forced a fumble, and picked off a pass. He scored twice . . . and he even blocked a punt! BYU won, 23–6.

CHICK-FIL-A BOWL
A clutch drive led by Clemson quarterback **Tajh Boyd** led to a game-winning kick. With less than two minutes left, Boyd rolled the Tigers into position for **Chandler Catanzaro** to kick a 37-yard field goal. Clemson beat LSU, 25–24, sparking off a huge celebration!

Clemson's Chandler Catanzaro gets a ride off the field after his bowl-game-winning kick.

Big Days and Big Plays!

College football in 2012 featured some amazing offensive performances. Players and teams put up huge point totals and records fell in many parts of the country. Here's a look at some of the more awesome offensive results.

Looks Like a Basketball Score!

The bad news was that Baylor lost Robert Griffin III to the pros. The good news was that new QB **Nick Florence** set a school record with 581 passing yards against West Virginia. The worse news was that West Virginia's **Geno Smith** did even better, throwing eight touchdown passes. The Mountaineers won a slugfest, 70–63.

Old Dominion . . . New Records

No one would blame quarterback **Taylor Heinicke** of Old Dominion if he said his arm was tired. He had given it quite a workout. Heinicke set NCAA Division 1 records against New Hampshire with 730 passing yards. By adding 61 rushing yards, he also set a total offense record. He needed every point he could get; Old Dominion won by only three points, 64–61.

Records Out West

✳ USC receiver **Marqise Lee** had a spectacular day when the Trojans played Arizona. Lee's 345 receiving yards were the most ever by a Pac-12 player.

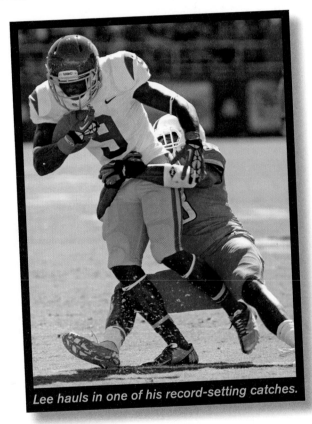
Lee hauls in one of his record-setting catches.

He had 16 catches and scored twice. However, Arizona upset USC, 39–36.

✳ A new rushing record was also set in the Pac-12. Arizona's **Ka'Deem Carey** bulled for 366 yards and five touchdowns, while leading the Wildcats to a 56–31 win over Colorado. The five scores were also a school record.

A Very Busy Guy

About the only thing that **Tavon Austin** didn't do for West Virginia against Oklahoma was punt. The running back ran for 344 yards and two touchdowns. He caught four passes for 82 yards. He barely had time to catch his breath, however, as he also returned kicks, adding 146 yards to reach an impressive total of 572 all-purpose yards. Austin's heroics were not enough, however. West Virginia lost, 50–49.

Most College Touchdowns—Ever

In more than 100 years of college football, no player has scored more touchdowns than Wisconsin's **Montee Ball**. He broke Barry Sanders's record and ended his amazing career with 83 total scores. The All-American is sure to find a happy home with an NFL team soon!

Too Bad Someone Had to Lose

In recent seasons, the matchup between USC and Oregon has always created fireworks. The 2012 edition was no different. It seemed for a while as if either team could score at will. In the end, Oregon's awesome offense was the difference. Running back **Kenjon Barner** was the star. He set an Oregon record with 321 rushing yards and scored five touchdowns. QB **Marcus Mariota** chipped in with four TD passes. USC's **Matt Barkley** had five of his own scoring passes, but they were not enough, and the Ducks quacked last, 62–51.

Wisconsin's Montee Ball doing what he did better than anyone else—score touchdowns!

Defense Had Its Day

Offense grabbed most of the headlines, but here are some big defensive moments from the 2012 season.

Goal-Line Stand ▶

Notre Dame's undefeated record was in trouble. Stanford was a yard away from a go-ahead score in overtime and had four tries to get in. The Fighting Irish, led by linebacker **Manti Te'o** rose up and stuffed Cardinal runners four times.

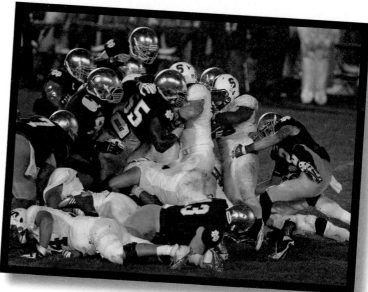

What a Hit!

South Carolina had just given up the football after nearly earning a first down. On the next play, South Carolina's **Jadeveon Clowney** smacked into Michigan's **Vincent Smith**. The tackle knocked off Smith's helmet and caused a fumble that South Carolina picked up. Clowney was later named to the All-American team.

Lying Down on the Job

Virginia Tech safety **Michael Cole** thought he was out of the play against Clemson when he slipped and fell. A moment later, he saw the ball flying by and reached up and grabbed it. He made the interception while he was flat on the ground!

PERFECT TOO LATE

The only major college team to finish the season undefeated didn't have a chance at the national championship. Ohio State went 12–0 and would have earned a spot in the Rose Bowl or even the BCS National Championship Game. However, the school was punished by the NCAA for breaking rules about accepting gifts in 2010. The 2012 team piled up win after win but was not eligible for championship or bowl games. The Buckeyes ended up ranked third in the nation, but had nothing to show for it.

2012 Numbers

42 TOUCHDOWN PASSES
◀◀◀ **Geno Smith**, West Virginia

4,309 PASSING YARDS
Nick Florence, Baylor

1,929 RUSHING YARDS
Ka'Deem Carey, Arizona

118 RECEPTIONS
Marqise Lee, USC

1,832 RECEIVING YARDS
Terrance Williams, Baylor

28 TOUCHDOWNS
Kenneth Dixon, Louisiana Tech

28 FIELD GOALS
Quinn Sharp, Oklahoma State

166 TACKLES
Dan Molls, Toledo

8 INTERCEPTIONS
Phillip Thomas, Fresno State

209

Fans at the September Louisiana Tech/ Houston game got their money's worth. The two teams set an NCAA record for most plays.

JOHNNY FOOTBALL!

Remember a couple of years ago when **Cam Newton** was running and passing all over college football? He was a tall, strong veteran player when he did all that, leading Auburn to a national title and winning the Heisman Trophy. Guess what? Another kid did even better. **Johnny Manziel**, known now to everyone as "Johnny Football," put up Newton-like numbers and won the 2012 Heisman Trophy. And Johnny Football is only a freshman; he was the first first-year player to win the award. Manziel passed for 3,706 yards (1,000 more than Newton) and 26 touchdowns. On the ground, the elusive Texas A&M QB ran for 1,410 yards and scored 21 times (one more than Newton). Manziel also led A&M's huge upset of Alabama. Look for more big things from this young player in the coming years. No one has won consecutive Heismans since **Archie Griffin** in 1974–75!

NCAA AWARD WINNERS

The Heisman Trophy goes to the top overall player, but NCAA players have a shot at a host of other honors. Here are some of the key awards given out after the 2012 season:

AWARD	FOR	PLAYER, SCHOOL
Campbell Trophy	Scholar-athlete	**Barrett Jones**, Alabama
Fred Biletnikoff Award	Wide receiver	**Marqise Lee**, USC
Lou Groza Award	Kicker	**Cairo Santos**, Tulane
Home Depot Award	Coach	**Chip Kelly**, Oregon
Nagurski Award	Defensive player	**Manti Te'o**, Notre Dame
Outland Trophy	Interior lineman	**Luke Joeckel**, Texas A&M
Doak Walker Award	Running back	**Montee Ball**, Wisconsin

Conference Champs

ATLANTIC COAST
Florida State

BIG 12
Kansas State

BIG EAST
Louisville

BIG TEN
Wisconsin

CONFERENCE USA
Tulsa

MID-AMERICAN
Northern Illinois

MOUNTAIN WEST
Boise State

PAC-12
Stanford

SEC
Alabama

SUN BELT
Arkansas State

WESTERN ATHLETIC
Utah State

Stanford head coach David Shaw smelled the Rose Bowl after winning the Pac-12.

OTHER NCAA CHAMPIONS

Alabama got all the attention, but other teams were champions, too. Here are the results of the other NCAA division championship games.

FCS

North Dakota St. 39, Sam Houston St. 13

North Dakota won its second straight title in a rematch of the 2011 game.

Division II

Valdosta St. 35, Winston-Salem 7

Valdosta won its third national title since 2004

Division III

Mt. Union 28, St. Thomas 10

This was Mt. Union's eighth straight title game appearance and 16th overall. This was their 11th title.

LUCKY 2013?

The Bowl Championship Series has not made many people happy. The BCS ends up with the BCS Championship Game, No. 1 vs. No. 2. But many fans still want a playoff, as the NCAA does in almost every other sport. The 2013 season will be the **final one** for the "old" BCS. Beginning in 2014, a "final four" of college teams will meet in semifinals and a final. The NCAA announced that the name of this new system will be The College Football Playoff. Okay, it's not that exciting, but maybe the games will be! The first championship under the new system will come after the 2014 season. The game will be on January 15, 2014, at Cowboys Stadium near Dallas.

2013 NCAA CHAMPION

Three NCAA championships in a row? That would be a tremendous feat. In fact, it's never been done, but we think it's about time. With many of its top players returning and with superstar coach **NICK SABAN** still on the sidelines, we think that the Crimson Tide will roll again. Our fearless prediction for the 2013 BCS Champion:

★ ALABAMA ★

We're No.1!

These are the teams that have finished at the top of the Associated Press's final rankings since the poll was first introduced in 1936.

SEASON	TEAM	RECORD	SEASON	TEAM	RECORD
2012	Alabama	13–1	1973	Notre Dame	11–0
2011	Alabama	12–1	1972	USC	12–0
2010	Auburn	14–0	1971	Nebraska	13–0
2009	Alabama	14–0	1970	Nebraska	11–0–1
2008	Florida	13–1	1969	Texas	11–0
2007	LSU	12–2	1968	Ohio State	10–0
2006	Florida	13–1	1967	USC	10–1
2005	Texas	13–0	1966	Notre Dame	9–0–1
2004	USC	13–0	1965	Alabama	9–1–1
2003	USC	12–1	1964	Alabama	10–1
2002	Ohio State	14–0	1963	Texas	11–0
2001	Miami	12–0	1962	USC	11–0
2000	Oklahoma	13–0	1961	Alabama	11–0
1999	Florida State	12–0	1960	Minnesota	8–2
1998	Tennessee	13–0	1959	Syracuse	11–0
1997	Michigan	12–0	1958	LSU	11–0
1996	Florida	12–1	1957	Auburn	10–0
1995	Nebraska	12–0	1956	Oklahoma	10–0
1994	Nebraska	13–0	1955	Oklahoma	11–0
1993	Florida State	12–1	1954	Ohio State	10–0
1992	Alabama	13–0	1953	Maryland	10–1
1991	Miami	12–0	1952	Michigan State	9–0
1990	Colorado	11–1–1	1951	Tennessee	10–1
1989	Miami	11–1	1950	Oklahoma	10–1
1988	Notre Dame	12–0	1949	Notre Dame	10–0
1987	Miami	12–0	1948	Michigan	9–0
1986	Penn State	12–0	1947	Notre Dame	9–0
1985	Oklahoma	11–1	1946	Notre Dame	8–0–1
1984	Brigham Young	13–0	1945	Army	9–0
1983	Miami	11–1	1944	Army	9–0
1982	Penn State	11–1	1943	Notre Dame	9–1
1981	Clemson	12–0	1942	Ohio State	9–1
1980	Georgia	12–0	1941	Minnesota	8–0
1979	Alabama	12–0	1940	Minnesota	8–0
1978	Alabama	11–1	1939	Texas A&M	11–0
1977	Notre Dame	11–1	1938	Texas Christian	11–0
1976	Pittsburgh	12–0	1937	Pittsburgh	9–0–1
1975	Oklahoma	11–1	1936	Minnesota	7–1
1974	Oklahoma	11–0			

BOWL CHAMPIONSHIP SERIES
NATIONAL CHAMPIONSHIP GAMES

College football (at its highest level) is one of the few sports that doesn't have an on-field playoff to determine its champion. In the 1998 season, the NCAA introduced the Bowl Championship Series (BCS), which pits the top two teams in the title game according to a complicated formula that takes into account records, polls, and computer rankings. At the end of the regular season, the No. 1 and No. 2 teams meet in a championship game.

SEASON	SCORE	SITE
2012	Alabama 42, Notre Dame 14	MIAMI, FL
2011	Alabama 21, LSU 0	NEW ORLEANS, LA
2010	Auburn 22, Oregon 19	GLENDALE, AZ
2009	Alabama 37, Texas 21	PASADENA, CA
2008	Florida 24, Oklahoma 14	MIAMI, FL
2007	LSU 38, Ohio State 24	NEW ORLEANS, LA
2006	Florida 41, Ohio State 14	GLENDALE, AZ
2005	Texas 41, USC 38	PASADENA, CA
2004	USC 55, Oklahoma 19	MIAMI, FL
2003	LSU 21, Oklahoma 14	NEW ORLEANS, LA
2002	Ohio State 31, Miami 24	TEMPE, AZ
2001	Miami 37, Nebraska 14	PASADENA, CA
2000	Oklahoma 13, Florida State 2	MIAMI, FL
1999	Florida State 46, Virginia Tech 29	NEW ORLEANS, LA
1998	Tennessee 23, Florida State 16	TEMPE, AZ

MLB

ONE MO TIME!
Mariano "Mo" Rivera has provided many thrilling moments in his amazing career, which ended after the 2013 season. He added another at the 2013 All-Star Game. Before he pitched the eighth inning, the best closer ever was alone on the field, bathed in the cheers of the fans at Citi Field as well as the applause of all the players on both teams. As the ovation went on and on, Rivera, the last player in the Majors to wear Jackie Robinson's retired No. 42, waved his hat in thanks. But most fans would agree, it should be thank you, Mo.

A Giant Surprise

Every baseball season includes a ton of surprises. The 2012 MLB campaign was no different. Several teams that were not expected to do well . . . did! And some teams with high hopes found them dashed.

The Baltimore Orioles were one of the most surprising teams of the year. Without a roster packed with All-Stars, the Orioles won close game after close game. They had a knack for finding that extra run or that out-of-nowhere pitch at just the right moment. They ended up 29–9 in games decided by one run. The O's were way behind the Yankees, trailing by as many as 13 games. But they kept plugging, and by the final day of the season, they had earned a spot in the wild-card playoff.

Almost as surprising was the fall of the Texas Rangers. After winning two straight AL championships, Texas looked primed for another in 2012. But they were overtaken by another surprise team, the Oakland Athletics. Needing only to beat Oakland on the final day, Texas collapsed.

> **❝Everyone says the A's can't compete. . . .we're better off if we're down. It just gives us extra energy.❞** — OAKLAND'S DEREK NORRIS

The A's, meanwhile, ended up winning the AL West with a final-game victory. The Rangers' nosedive continued in the playoffs, where the O's sent them home early. With the lowest payroll in the game, the A's proved you don't have to be rich to win. Ask the Boston Red Sox about that. They're the third highest spending team, paying their players very large sums. But after slipping in 2011, they crashed in 2012. With only 63 wins, the team posted its worst record

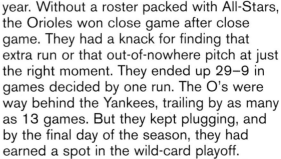

The surprising Orioles jumped right into the playoffs!

2012 FINAL STANDINGS

AL EAST

Yankees	95–67
Orioles	93–69
Rays	90–72
Blue Jays	73–89
Red Sox	69–93

AL CENTRAL

Tigers	88–74
White Sox	85–77
Royals	72–90
Indians	68–94
Twins	66–96

AL WEST

Athletics	94–68
Rangers	93–69
Angels	89–73
Mariners	75–87

NL EAST

Nationals	98–64
Braves	94–68
Phillies	81–81
Mets	74–88
Marlins	69–93

NL CENTRAL

Reds	97–65
Cardinals	88–74
Brewers	83–79
Pirates	79–83
Cubs	61–101
Astros	55–107

NL WEST

Giants	94–68
Dodgers	86–76
Diamondbacks	81–81
Padres	76–86
Rockies	64–98

since 1965! New manager **John Farrell** takes over in 2013, so Boston fans are hopeful their team will find the magic again.

Over in the NL, the Washington Nationals surprised everyone but their fans by putting up the league's best record. They were led by a trio of great young pitchers— **Gio Gonzalez**, **Jordan Zimmerman**, and **Stephen Strasburg**. Strasburg was the center of one of the year's biggest stories. Though he can reach 100 mph with his fastball, he was coming off arm surgery. The Nats decided to have him stop pitching after 160 innings, no matter how the team was doing. As they charged toward the playoffs, many experts were surprised that Washington stuck to its plan. Strasburg stopped pitching in early September. Still, the Nats made it to the NLDS, but were upset by the Cardinals.

The Giants were the steadiest team in the NL, taking over their division lead and cruising to the playoffs. Once there, San Francisco's great starting pitching took over. Even when facing the hard-hitting Detroit Tigers in the World Series, the Giants stood tall on the mound. With a quick four-game sweep, they took home the championship for the second time in three years.

.763

The Orioles' winning percentage in one-run games was the best since the 1890 Brooklyn Bridegrooms (.778).

The Playoffs!

Wild-Card Playoffs

For the first time, MLB held a wild-card playoff. The top two second-place teams met in a one-game showdown. The winners earn a spot in the League Division Series. Matching their name, the wild-card games were both pretty . . . wild!

AL WILD CARD
Baltimore 5, Texas 1

The Orioles made the most of their first postseason spot in 15 seasons. Pitcher **Joe** **Saunders** kept the powerful Rangers bats quiet. The Orioles chipped away at Rangers ace **Yu Darvish** and headed into the next round.

NL WILD CARD
St. Louis 6, Atlanta 3

Three Atlanta errors helped the Cardinals take the lead early. A controversial call by an umpire angered Atlanta fans later. They delayed the game 19 minutes after throwing trash on the field! But the defending World Series champion Cardinals escaped to play again.

Divisional Playoffs

NATIONAL LEAGUE
St. Louis vs. Washington

The Nationals' great pitching helped them win Game 1, but then the Cardinals roared back with a pair of big wins. St. Louis scored 20 runs total in Games 2 and 3. Outfielder **Carlos Beltran** led the way with a pair of homers. In Game 4, however, the Nats tied the series on **Jayson Werth**'s walk-off homer. Game 5 had drama, too. As Nats fans looked on, stunned, St. Louis scored four runs in the ninth

Pete Kozma drove in the winner for St. Louis.

inning to rally for a 9–7 win. The Cardinals had been down by as many as six runs earlier in the game. It was the biggest comeback ever in an elimination game.

San Francisco vs. Cincinnati

The Giants overcame three RBI by Cincinnati's **Brandon Phillips** for a Game 1 win. Cincy struck back in Game 2, as pitcher **Bronson Arroyo** allowed only two hits. The Giants bounced back with a win in Game 3 and then great pitching by **Tim Lincecum** tied the Series at two games apiece. In Game 5, the catcher **Buster Posey** hit a grand slam that helped the Giants return to the NLCS.

AMERICAN LEAGUE
Baltimore vs. N.Y. Yankees

The bullpen, a strength for the Orioles, turned into a weakness in Game 1. Closer **Jim Johnson** gave up five runs in the ninth to let the Yankees win. In his first postseason game, Baltimore's **Wei-Yin Chin** won Game 2. Game 3 provided drama, as New York's **Raul Ibanez** tied the game with a homer in the ninth, then won it with another in the 12th. Game 4 was another extra-inning thriller, but this time the O's came out on top in 13. Baltimore's season ended in Game 5, as Yankees ace **C. C. Sabathia** shut them down.

Sabathia closed out the O's in New York.

Detroit vs. Oakland

Detroit took Game 1 thanks to a great job by ace **Justin Verlander**. In Game 2, Detroit's **Don Kelley** hit a walk-off sac fly for the victory. But Oakland's pitchers threw a shutout in Game 3. Facing the end of their season in Game 4, the A's scored three runs in the bottom of the ninth. **Coco Crisp**'s walk-off single tied the series. But Verlander was too much again in Game 5, striking out 11 A's as the Tigers won, 6–0.

2012 Championship Series

NATIONAL LEAGUE
St. Louis vs. San Francisco

In Game 1, a pair of Cardinals hitters who were already playoff heroes did it again. **David Freese**, the 2011 World Series MVP, and **Carlos Beltran** each had homers as St. Louis won. In Game 2, a trio of Giants had two hits each as their team evened the series. A rain delay in Game 3 helped the Cardinals settle down and win at home. Every starter had a hit as the Cardinals smacked around Giants pitchers to take a 3–1 lead in games. But San Francisco was not done yet. Over the next three games, San Francisco pitchers allowed only one run, throwing a pair of shutouts in Games 5 and 7. The comeback, one of the best ever in the NLCS, gave the Giants a chance at their second World Series title in three years.
Giants 4–Cardinals 3
NLCS MVP: Marco Scutaro, Giants

AMERICAN LEAGUE
Detroit vs. N.Y. Yankees

Game 1 in this battle for the AL title included drama and a tough break. First, the Yankees rallied with four runs in the bottom of the ninth to tie the game, helped by another **Raul Ibanez** homer. In the 12th, though, the Yanks lost captain and shortstop **Derek Jeter**, who broke his ankle making a diving stop. A few moments later, they lost the game, too, as **Delmon Young**'s double was the difference. In Game 2, the Yanks missed Jeter and a lot of pitches from **Anibel Sanchez**, who gave up just three hits in seven innings. Young had a key RBI again in the Tigers' shutout. The Tigers kept roaring in Game 3, thanks to Justin Verlander winning his third game of the 2012 postseason. Young had his fifth RBI of the series. Detroit wrapped up a sweep with a four-homer, 8–1 thrashing of the Yanks. The win sent Detroit to the World Series for the first time since they lost to St. Louis in 2006.
Tigers 4–Yankees 0
ALCS MVP: Delmon Young, Tigers

Young slugged the Tigers to the World Series.

2012 World Series

The Giants won it all, making it their second World Series title in three seasons. San Francisco bottled up the powerful Tigers' offense and won four straight games. Meanwhile, another kind of mammal rose to national fame. Make way for Panda Power!

GAME 1: Giants 8–Tigers 3

The first three times that Giants third baseman **Pablo Sandoval** came to bat, he hit a homer! The player nicknamed "Kung Fu Panda" became only the fourth player ever with three homers in a World Series game. (**Babe Ruth** did it in 1926 and 1928, **Reggie Jackson** in 1977, and **Albert Pujols** in 2011.) That power display was more than enough to lead the Giants to a win. In the third inning, however, they also got a lucky bounce. A ball hit by **Angel Pagan** hit third base to keep a rally alive.

GAME 2: Giants 2–Tigers 0

Another bit of luck helped the Giants in Game 2. A seventh-inning bunt by **Gregor Blanco** hugged the third-base line. It rolled to a stop as a pair of Tigers watched. The hit led to the first run of the game. That would be all that Giants starter **Madison Bumgarner** would need. He allowed only three hits and three walks in seven innings.

GAME 3: Giants 2–Tigers 0

Great pitching was the key to the Giants' third straight win.

Ryan Vogelsong and **Tim Lincecum** caged the Tigers. The Giants' lucky play came in the second inning. On a 3-2 count, Gregor Blanco swung and got just a tiny bit of the ball, enough to foul it off. He tripled on the next pitch to drive in the first run. A swing and a miss there and who knows what happens? Everything was rolling the Giants way.

GAME 4: Giants 4–Tigers 3

It took an extra inning, but the result was the same, and San Francisco won the World Series trophy. Series MVP **Marco Scutaro** drove in the winning run for the Giants. Closer **Sergio Romo** came on again to shut the door on the Tigers for his third save of the Series. It was the Giants' ninth all-time.

Sandoval put on a Series power surge in Game 1.

Award Winners

MOST VALUABLE PLAYER
AL: **MIGUEL CABRERA**, TIGERS
NL: **BUSTER POSEY**, GIANTS

CY YOUNG AWARD
AL: **DAVID PRICE**, RAYS
NL: **R. A. DICKEY**, METS

ROOKIE OF THE YEAR
AL: **MIKE TROUT**, ANGELS
NL: **BRYCE HARPER**, NATIONALS

MANAGER OF THE YEAR
AL: **BOB MELVIN**, ATHLETICS
NL: **DAVEY JOHNSON**, NATIONALS

HANK AARON AWARD
AL: **MIGUEL CABRERA**, TIGERS
NL: **BUSTER POSEY**, GIANTS

ROBERTO CLEMENTE AWARD
(for community service)
CLAYTON KERSHAW, DODGERS

Price won 20 games for Tampa Bay and also led the AL with a 2.56 ERA.

Stat Champs

AL Hitting Leaders

44 HOME RUNS
139 RBI
.330 BATTING AVERAGE
Miguel Cabrera, Tigers

49 STOLEN BASES
Mike Trout, Angels

216 HITS
Derek Jeter, Yankees

NL Hitting Leaders

41 HOME RUNS
Ryan Braun, Brewers

115 RBI
Chase Headley, Padres

.336 BATTING AVERAGE
Buster Posey, Giants ▶ ▶ ▶

44 STOLEN BASES
Everth Cabrera, Padres

194 HITS
Andrew McCutchen, Pirates

AL Pitching Leaders

20 WINS
David Price, Rays
Jered Weaver, Angels

51 SAVES
Jim Johnson, Orioles

2.56 ERA
David Price, Rays

239 STRIKEOUTS
Justin Verlander, Tigers

NL Pitching Leaders

21 WINS
Gio Gonzalez, Nationals

42 SAVES
Craig Kimbrel, Braves
Jason Motte, Cardinals

2.53 ERA
Clayton Kershaw, Dodgers

230 STRIKEOUTS
R.A. Dickey, Mets

2012 Highlights

Titanic Tiger!

The hitting Triple Crown in baseball is one of the rarest feats in the game. In order to do so, a player must lead the league in homers, RBI, and average. This hadn't happened since **Carl Yastrzemski** did it in 1967. In 2012, Detroit's **Miguel Cabrera** finally broke through. The slugging third baseman led the AL with 44 homers, 139 RBI, and a .330 batting average. He had his toughest battle for the top home-run spot, as **Curtis Granderson** and **Josh Hamilton** each had 43 dingers.

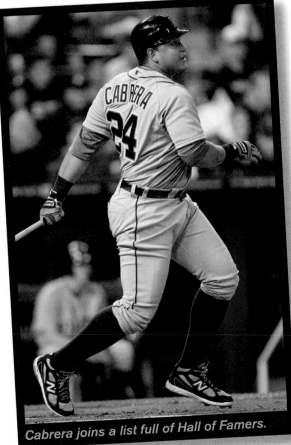

Cabrera joins a list full of Hall of Famers.

Ten Most Recent Triple Crown Winners

2012	**Miguel Cabrera**,	Tigers
1967	**Carl Yastrzemski**,	Red Sox
1966	**Frank Robinson**,	Orioles
1956	**Mickey Mantle**,	Yankees
1947	**Ted Williams**,	Red Sox
1942	**Ted Williams**,	Red Sox
1937	**Joe Medwick**,	Cardinals
1934	**Lou Gehrig**,	Yankees
1933	**Jimmie Foxx**,	Athletics
1933	**Chuck Klein**,	Phillies

GOOD-BYE, CHIPPER

One of the most popular players in baseball hung up his glove in 2012. Third baseman **Chipper Jones** played 19 seasons with Atlanta, helping them win 11 division titles and the 1995 World Series. He was the MVP in 1999 and slugged 468 homers. That's the third-most home runs ever by a switch-hitter. Jones started out as a number-one draft pick in 1990. He ended up as the Braves' all-time leader in many categories, as well as with a reputation as a great clubhouse leader. Next stop: Cooperstown.

Amazing Angel!

Baseball scouts like to talk about "tools." Those are the key skills that great ballplayers should have—hitting for power and for average, throwing arm, great fielding, and baserunning. A "five-tool" player excels at every part of the game. **Mike Trout**, the Angels' amazing rookie outfielder, has all those tools . . . and more. In 2012, he became the first player in history to bat .320 while hitting 30 homers and stealing 45 bases (he had 49). And get this: Trout only turned 21 on August 7, 2012! He not only won Rookie of the Year, but also finished second to **Miguel Cabrera** for MVP. The sky is truly the limit for this Angel.

STRIKEOUT NEWS

While big hitters got all the headlines, strikeouts made the record books, from both pitchers and hitters.

* Detroit's **Doug Fister** struck out nine straight Royals on September 27, a new big-league record.

* Five Angels struck out 20 Mariners on September 25. Two pitchers—**Roger Clemens** and **Kerry Wood**—had done that, but no group of pitchers ever had.

* **Adam Dunn** struck out at an amazing pace. In 2012, he was the first player ever with back-to-back seasons with twice as many Ks as hits.

000 000 000

2012: A YEAR OF NO-NOS

The 2012 season saw an amazing seven no-hitters, one of the highest single-season totals ever. Here are the details:

DATE	PITCHER, TEAM	OPPONENT	SCORE
4/21	**Philip Humber**, White Sox	Mariners	4–0*
5/2	**Jered Weaver**, Angels	Twins	9–0
6/1	**Johan Santana**, Mets	Cardinals	8–0
6/8	**Six Mariners pitchers**	Dodgers	1–0
6/13	**Matt Cain**, Giants	Astros	10–0*
8/15	**Felix Hernandez**, Mariners	Rays	1–0*
9/28	**Homer Bailey**, Reds	Pirates	1–0

* Perfect games; first season ever with three

Baseball 2013

News and notes from around the Major Leagues for the first half of the 2013 season.

Prince Fielder is one of baseball's biggest sluggers. So it was appropriate that the Topps Company chose him to grace the world's largest baseball card. At 90 feet by 60 feet, it was displayed in Florida during Spring Training.

as the only players ever with dingers in the season's first four games. It was also the most RBI in that span ever. By late July, Davis was still hot, leading the majors in homers.

✳ In May, calls for more and better instant replay in baseball were loud after a game-winning home run by Oakland's **Adam Rosales** was ruled a double. The video seemed to show clearly that the ball was over the fence, but umps said otherwise . . . even after watching TV! Look for baseball to keep trying to improve its replay rules in 2014 and beyond.

✳ The Houston Astros joined the American League in 2013. The Astros had been part of the National League since their first season in 1962. (Trivia time: The team was called the Houston Colt .45s until 1965.) Moving to a new league didn't help, as the 'Stros were at the bottom of their new home in the AL West.

✳ Baltimore 1B **Chris Davis** blasted out of the gate in 2013. In his first four games, he was 9 for 15 with 4 homers and 16 RBI! He joins Willie Mays, Mark McGwire, and Nelson Cruz

✳ Mariano Rivera (page 58 and right) was the big story and the MVP of the 2013 All-Star Game. However, the news was also good for the AL. Its 3–0 win gave it home-field advantage in the World Series.

Hello, Yasiel!

Remember **Jeremy Lin**? He was the out-of-nowhere player who lit up the NBA in the spring of 2012. In the spring of 2013, baseball had its own version. Cuban sensation **Yasiel Puig** jumped from Double-A to the Dodgers in early June and proceeded to tear up big-league pitching. In his first 15 games, he hit .474 with five homers and 11 RBI. He also had 27 hits in those games, a mark topped only twice since 1901! Puig had a grand slam in his second game, and hit a homer on his first visit to Yankee Stadium. He also ended a game by doubling up a runner at first with a peg from the warning track. You might be watching the game's next superstar . . . he certainly got off to a fast start!

GOODBYE, MARIANO!

The greatest closer in baseball history said that 2013 would be his last season. **Mariano Rivera** of the Yankees was dominant in the playoffs and World Series, racking up 42 saves and a 0.70 ERA (through 2012). But he was just as powerful in the regular season. He had more saves than anyone else, thanks to his longevity and his amazing cutter, which he threw more than 90 percent of the time. Even though hitters knew it was coming, its late movement was so tricky that he fooled the game's greats time and again. Rivera is a lock for the Hall of Fame in five years, a fantastic pitcher and a great gentleman of the game.

WORLD BASEBALL CLASSIC

For the first time, the World Baseball Classic trophy won't make the trip across the Pacific Ocean. Japan won the first two WBCs, but in 2013, the Dominican Republic won it for the first time (above). In an all-Caribbean final played in San Diego, the D.R. defeated Puerto Rico, 3–0. The champions were a perfect 8-0 in the tournament that matched the national teams of the world's best baseball nations.

Japan did make the semifinals, but lost to Puerto Rico. The surprise team of the tournament was the Netherlands, which made it to the semifinals as well. It's worth noting, however, that almost all of the Dutch players were from the Netherlands Antilles, a Caribbean island colony. Former MLB slugger **Andruw Jones** and top prospect **Jurickson Profar** played a big part in the the Dutch rise.

The champions used a host of All-Star Major Leaguers to earn the title. **Robinson Cano** (Yankees), **Carlos Santana** (Indians), **Nelson Cruz** (Rangers), **Hanley Ramirez** (Dodgers), and **Edwin Encarnacion** (Blue Jays) were just some of the big-league sluggers who made their island home happy.

THE CARIBBEAN SERIES

While the Dominican Republic took home the WBC trophy, a team from that country missed out on the Caribbean Series title. The Mexican League's **Obregon Yaquis** beat the D.R.'s **Escogido Leones** to win the annual championship of Caribbean pro baseball leagues. The Yaquis had to go a long way to win. The 18-inning final took more than seven hours to complete! The Leones first had to come back in the 14th after the Yaquis took the lead in the top of the inning. Then, four innings later, a home run by **Douglas Clark** snapped a 3–3 tie and the Yaquis held on to win. It was the seventh time a team from Mexico won the Caribbean Series.

2014: Rookies to Watch

MARK APPEL, P, ASTROS
The No. 1 draft pick in 2013, he's expected to have a fast rise to the Majors. A standout college pitcher with great speed and size, Appel will help the pitching-poor Astros.

BILLY HAMILTON, OF, REDS ▶▶▶
Cincinnati can't wait to get this guy's speed on the field. In 2012, he stole an amazing 155 bases. In Triple A in 2013, he was on his way to another 100.

OSCAR TAVERAS, OF, CARDINALS
One report called him the "best pure hitter in the minor leagues." St. Louis has a crowded outfield, but this young star might force his way into their lineup.

The Empty Hall

For the first time since 1996, the Baseball Writers Association did not choose any players for the Baseball Hall of Fame. Some of the game's biggest names were on the list, but the writers knew or suspected several of having used performance-enhancing drugs. **Barry Bonds**, **Roger Clemens**, **Mike Piazza**, **Mark McGwire**, and **Sammy Sosa** were among the record-setting stars who were denied a place in the Hall. All were connected with PEDs, and voters felt that such people were not Hall-worthy. The players will have more chances in the years ahead, but it was a bold move by the writers this time around.

The Veterans Committee did choose three inductees: 1890s catcher **Deacon White**, 1920s umpire **Hank O'Day**, and longtime Yankees owner **Jacob Ruppert**.

2013 WORLD SERIES

Our Fearless Prediction: We're excited by the midseason form of the Red Sox and Pirates, but with another team's experiences pitching staff and solid defense make them our pick for the 2013 World Series champ:

ST. LOUIS ★ CARDINALS ★

World Series Winners

YEAR	WINNER	RUNNER-UP	SCORE*	YEAR	WINNER	RUNNER-UP	SCORE*
2012	San Francisco Giants	Detroit Tigers	4-0	1986	New York Mets	Boston Red Sox	4-3
2011	St. Louis Cardinals	Texas Rangers	4-3	1985	Kansas City Royals	St. Louis Cardinals	4-3
2010	San Francisco Giants	Texas Rangers	4-1	1984	Detroit Tigers	San Diego Padres	4-1
2009	New York Yankees	Philadelphia Phillies	4-2	1983	Baltimore Orioles	Philadelphia Phillies	4-1
2008	Philadelphia Phillies	Tampa Bay Rays	4-1	1982	St. Louis Cardinals	Milwaukee Brewers	4-3
2007	Boston Red Sox	Colorado Rockies	4-0	1981	Los Angeles Dodgers	New York Yankees	4-2
2006	St. Louis Cardinals	Detroit Tigers	4-1	1980	Philadelphia Phillies	Kansas City Royals	4-2
2005	Chicago White Sox	Houston Astros	4-0	1979	Pittsburgh Pirates	Baltimore Orioles	4-3
2004	Boston Red Sox	St. Louis Cardinals	4-0	1978	New York Yankees	Los Angeles Dodgers	4-2
2003	Florida Marlins	New York Yankees	4-2	1977	New York Yankees	Los Angeles Dodgers	4-2
2002	Anaheim Angels	San Francisco Giants	4-3	1976	Cincinnati Reds	New York Yankees	4-0
2001	Arizona Diamondbacks	New York Yankees	4-3	1975	Cincinnati Reds	Boston Red Sox	4-3
2000	New York Yankees	New York Mets	4-1	1974	Oakland Athletics	Los Angeles Dodgers	4-1
1999	New York Yankees	Atlanta Braves	4-0	1973	Oakland Athletics	New York Mets	4-3
1998	New York Yankees	San Diego Padres	4-0	1972	Oakland Athletics	Cincinnati Reds	4-3
1997	Florida Marlins	Cleveland Indians	4-3	1971	Pittsburgh Pirates	Baltimore Orioles	4-3
1996	New York Yankees	Atlanta Braves	4-2	1970	Baltimore Orioles	Cincinnati Reds	4-1
1995	Atlanta Braves	Cleveland Indians	4-2	1969	New York Mets	Baltimore Orioles	4-1
1993	Toronto Blue Jays	Philadelphia Phillies	4-2	1968	Detroit Tigers	St. Louis Cardinals	4-3
1992	Toronto Blue Jays	Atlanta Braves	4-2	1967	St. Louis Cardinals	Boston Red Sox	4-3
1991	Minnesota Twins	Atlanta Braves	4-3	1966	Baltimore Orioles	Los Angeles Dodgers	4-0
1990	Cincinnati Reds	Oakland Athletics	4-0	1965	Los Angeles Dodgers	Minnesota Twins	4-3
1989	Oakland Athletics	San Francisco Giants	4-0	1964	St. Louis Cardinals	New York Yankees	4-3
1988	Los Angeles Dodgers	Oakland Athletics	4-1	1963	Los Angeles Dodgers	New York Yankees	4-0
1987	Minnesota Twins	St. Louis Cardinals	4-3	1962	New York Yankees	San Francisco Giants	4-3

* Score is represented in games played.

YEAR	WINNER	RUNNER-UP	SCORE*	YEAR	WINNER	RUNNER-UP	SCORE*
1961	New York Yankees	Cincinnati Reds	4-1	1932	New York Yankees	Chicago Cubs	4-0
1960	Pittsburgh Pirates	New York Yankees	4-3	1931	St. Louis Cardinals	Philadelphia Athletics	4-3
1959	Los Angeles Dodgers	Chicago White Sox	4-2	1930	Philadelphia Athletics	St. Louis Cardinals	4-2
1958	New York Yankees	Milwaukee Braves	4-3	1929	Philadelphia Athletics	Chicago Cubs	4-1
1957	Milwaukee Braves	New York Yankees	4-3	1928	New York Yankees	St. Louis Cardinals	4-0
1956	New York Yankees	Brooklyn Dodgers	4-3	1927	New York Yankees	Pittsburgh Pirates	4-0
1955	Brooklyn Dodgers	New York Yankees	4-3	1926	St. Louis Cardinals	New York Yankees	4-3
1954	New York Giants	Cleveland Indians	4-0	1925	Pittsburgh Pirates	Washington Senators	4-3
1953	New York Yankees	Brooklyn Dodgers	4-2	1924	Washington Senators	New York Giants	4-3
1952	New York Yankees	Brooklyn Dodgers	4-3	1923	New York Yankees	New York Giants	4-2
1951	New York Yankees	New York Giants	4-2	1922	New York Giants	New York Yankees	4-0
1950	New York Yankees	Philadelphia Phillies	4-0	1921	New York Giants	New York Yankees	5-3
1949	New York Yankees	Brooklyn Dodgers	4-1	1920	Cleveland Indians	Brooklyn Dodgers	5-2
1948	Cleveland Indians	Boston Braves	4-2	1919	Cincinnati Reds	Chicago White Sox	5-3
1947	New York Yankees	Brooklyn Dodgers	4-3	1918	Boston Red Sox	Chicago Cubs	4-2
1946	St. Louis Cardinals	Boston Red Sox	4-3	1917	Chicago White Sox	New York Giants	4-2
1945	Detroit Tigers	Chicago Cubs	4-3	1916	Boston Red Sox	Brooklyn Dodgers	4-1
1944	St. Louis Cardinals	St. Louis Browns	4-2	1915	Boston Red Sox	Philadelphia Phillies	4-1
1943	New York Yankees	St. Louis Cardinals	4-1	1914	Boston Braves	Philadelphia Athletics	4-0
1942	St. Louis Cardinals	New York Yankees	4-1	1913	Philadelphia Athletics	New York Giants	4-1
1941	New York Yankees	Brooklyn Dodgers	4-1	1912	Boston Red Sox	New York Giants	4-3
1940	Cincinnati Reds	Detroit Tigers	4-3	1911	Philadelphia Athletics	New York Giants	4-2
1939	New York Yankees	Cincinnati Reds	4-0	1910	Philadelphia Athletics	Chicago Cubs	4-1
1938	New York Yankees	Chicago Cubs	4-0	1909	Pittsburgh Pirates	Detroit Tigers	4-3
1937	New York Yankees	New York Giants	4-1	1908	Chicago Cubs	Detroit Tigers	4-1
1936	New York Yankees	New York Giants	4-2	1907	Chicago Cubs	Detroit Tigers	4-0
1935	Detroit Tigers	Chicago Cubs	4-2	1906	Chicago White Sox	Chicago Cubs	4-2
1934	St. Louis Cardinals	Detroit Tigers	4-3	1905	New York Giants	Philadelphia Athletics	4-1
1933	New York Giants	Washington Senators	4-1	1903	Boston Red Sox	Pittsburgh Pirates	5-3

Note: 1904 not played because NL-champion Giants refused to play; 1994 not played due to MLB work stoppage.

COLLEGE BASKETBALL

HAPPY HUSKIES!

The University of Connecticut has dominated women's basketball for more than a decade. In April 2013, they added to their legacy by winning their record-tying eighth NCAA championship. Their win capped an amazing month of March Madness for both men and women. Check out all the details on pages 82 and 85.

Musical Chairs

The name of the game was supposed to be college basketball, but the men's teams seemed like they were playing musical chairs! From the first tip-off in the fall of 2012 to the game-ending buzzer at the Final Four in April 2013, college hoops had more bounces than a room full of basketballs.

Team after team rose to No. 1 only to lose. Was the pressure of being at the top too much to handle? Teams ranked No. 1 lost six times during the season, one of the highest totals ever. Eighteen teams that were not ranked in the top 25 defeated teams ranked in the top five. That's the most since 2008.

Indiana was the first to fall, losing to unranked Butler in December. Then Duke tumbled from the top, followed by Louisville and then Michigan. On January 23, Duke was back on top but was crushed by Miami of Florida by 37 points. Miami's rise among the nation's best—they were ACC champs—was one of the big stories of this season.

Indiana was on top again in February. They thought they had an easy game against unranked Illinois. Nope: The Illini came back from being down 12 points at the half to stun the Hoosiers.

Indiana reached No. 1 again in February . . . but it didn't last—again. This time it was the Golden Gophers from the University of Minnesota that pulled the big upset. That left the door open for yet another team to rise to the top, but this one was a real newsmaker. Gonzaga, from Washington state, has been a good-but-not-great team for several seasons. But on Feb. 23, they earned their first-ever No. 1 ranking. It was also the first time since 2008 that a team not in one of the six major conferences was ranked that high. Of course, having reached No. 1, the 'Zags were upset early in the NCAA tournament by Wichita State.

The postseason conference tournaments brought even more surprises. Oregon stormed through to

Kelly Olynyk (left) led Gonzaga to its best season ever.

FINAL MEN'S TOP 10
USA Today Coaches Poll

1. Louisville
2. Michigan
3. Syracuse
4. Wichita State
5. Duke
6. Ohio State
7. Indiana
8. Kansas
9. Florida
10. Miami

win the Pac-12 over favored UCLA. Ohio State recovered from its earlier losses to win the hard-fought Big 10. In the always-tough Atlantic Coast Conference, Miami beat North Carolina for the title. In the final year of the Big East Conference, Louisville gave a hint of things to come, upsetting Syracuse to win the title.

With all the excitement of the regular season, fans expected a wide-open NCAA tournament—and they got one! Read all about it on page 82.

The final bounces came on April 8 when Louisville outlasted Michigan to win the national championship. Now that was a No. 1 that no one could take away from them!

Illinois (in white) surrounded Indiana and produced one of the season's many big upsets.

Hoop Notes

students after a big win. Some people even said it was happening too much and worried that someone might be hurt in the crowd. But as long as there are big wins and happy students, the courts will be stormed!

◄◄◄ The Game That Wouldn't End!

Notre Dame played Louisville on February 9 . . . and it almost went to February 10. The teams needed five overtime periods to decide the winner. Notre Dame outlasted Louisville to win 104–101. It was the longest regular-season game in Big East Conference history. "Unbelievable. I'm really proud of my team. Many times we were down in the overtimes and kept fighting back," Notre Dame coach **Mike Brey** said. "It's one of those magical nights."

Year of the Court Storming!

With all the upsets and the defeats of No. 1s (see page 78), college fans had a lot to celebrate this season. It seemed like every week that a court suddenly filled with celebrating

Sudden Victory!

In the Atlantic 10 conference tournament, Richmond led Charlotte by three points with five seconds left. Thanks to their coach, however, they ended up losing in one of the wildest finishes ever! First, after Charlotte made one

138

No, that's not the score for a whole team. That's how many **Jack Taylor** from Grinnell College scored in *one game*! Taylor started shooting and never stopped, setting a new NCAA record for points in a game. He took 108 shots and made 79. He even had seven free throws. (Yes, Grinnell won!)

An Un-Record

Normally, a school that set a pair of NCAA Division 1 scoring records would be pretty happy. But Northern Illinois would prefer not to be in the record books. On January 26, Northern Illinois scored only four points in the first half against Eastern Michigan. They ended up losing that game 42–25. The four-point half broke the record of five points . . . that Northern Illinois had set in December!

free throw, the refs called a technical foul on Richmond for a shove. That meant two more free throws. After another quick foul, Richmond coach **Chris Mooney** sort of went nuts. Screaming and throwing his jacket, he was called for two more technical fouls. As a result, Charlotte got *seven* more shots from the line, making four. Charlotte's **Pierria Henry** ended up making seven of 11 free-throw attempts with less than five seconds in the game. Ouch.

Top Player! ▶▶▶

In one of the closest votes ever, Michigan's **Trey Burke** won the Wooden Award as the top player in the country. The sophomore guard had just 90 more points in the voting than Indiana's **Victor Oladipo**. Burke averaged 18.8 points per game. He led Michigan to the national championship game, where they lost to Louisville.

March Madness!

The NCAA tournament always creates drama, excitement, and heartache. In 2013, the teams combined to make all that and much more. Here are some of the highlights:

▶ Harvard won its first-ever NCAA tournament game. Seeded No. 13, they stunned New Mexico in the first round.

Florida Gulf Coast flew high to shock favored Georgetown.

▶ Calling their hometown "Dunk City," Florida Gulf Coast University amazed fans with their high-flying skills. They upset No. 2–seed Georgetown to become the tournament's "Cinderella Team." With a second-round win over San Diego State, FGCU became the first No. 15 team to make the Sweet 16.

▶ Along with FGCU, teams seeded 12th (three teams), 13th (La Salle), and 14th (Harvard) also made the round of 32.

▶ Wichita State, a No. 9 seed, is called the Shockers. They were certainly shocking in upsetting Gonzaga and later making the Final Four.

▶ Buzzer-beaters: Ohio State needed game-winning three-point shots in back-to-back games to survive early-round games against Iowa State and Arizona. Michigan's **Trey Burke** made a three-point shot at the buzzer to tie Kansas. The Wolverines won in overtime in one of the tournament's best games.

▶ In Louisville's win over Duke, **Kevin Ware** of the Cardinals suffered a horrible broken leg. But he showed great courage by returning from surgery to cheer on his teammates, whom he called "his brothers."

FINAL FOUR

Louisville 72– Wichita State 68

The Cardinals' stirring comeback from being behind by 12 points prevented Wichita State from another shocking win.

Michigan 61–Syracuse 56

With a late chance to win, Syracuse was called for a key charging foul. Michigan held on for the big victory.

Cardinals Clinch It!

The Louisville Cardinals won their third national championship with a stirring 82–76 win over Michigan. A record crowd of 74,326 packed the Georgia Dome to watch the game. Everyone wanted to see a great game and the two teams delivered—big-time.

Inspired by their injured guard **Kevin Ware** (see page 82), Louisville came from behind several times. Their late-game 20–8 run helped hold off a final Michigan comeback.

Both teams played extremely well, and many experts called the game one of the best ever in a final. For Louisville, **Kevin Hancock** (shooting in photo) was the hot hand, scoring a team-high 22 points. For Michigan, **Spike Albrecht** was nearly as good, making four big three-point shots in the first half. One sequence showed how hot the action was. The two teams had back-to-back alley-oop baskets that brought the huge crowd to its feet. First Louisville's **Peyton Siva** rose up for a layup. On the next play, **Glen Robinson** slammed home a lob for Michigan.

A big turning point late in the game came when a Michigan player stepped out of bounds. Then Louisville's clutch free throws sealed the win.

Best Day Ever

For Louisville coach **Rick Pitino**, April 9 might have been the best day he has ever had:

→ his son was named head coach at Minnesota

→ he got a $2.7 million bonus from Louisville

→ he was elected to the Basketball Hall of Fame

→ his team won the national championship

Wow!

2012-13 Women's Hoops

The story of women's college basketball was one thing in the regular season, and a very different one in the NCAA tournament. Unlike the men's season, the top women's teams stayed on top.

The season began with Baylor as defending champ and riding a long winning streak. That streak ended at 42 games with a loss to Stanford in November. But led by megastar **Brittney Griner**, Baylor started another streak, winning their next 32 straight. Stanford itself was later upset in its conference tourney by the University of California at Berkeley.

Meanwhile, seven-time champ Connecticut and Notre Dame met three times during the season. Connecticut lost all three times! Notre Dame was led by point guard **Skylar Diggins**. Her all-around game was too much for UConn to handle. On March 4, the two teams battled through three overtimes to decide a winner. Diggins played every minute and led both teams with 29 points in her last home game at Notre Dame. After an exhausting evening, the Fighting Irish ended up on top, 96–87.

The excitement of the regular season set fans up for a rollicking NCAA tournament.

Griner set a record for most dunks (18).

BEST EVER?

By the time you read this, **Brittney Griner** will be a rising star in the WNBA. But most experts agree that she was also the greatest women's college player ever. In four years at Baylor, she scored the second-most points all-time, while setting all-time career marks for blocks and dunks. She led Baylor to the 2012 national championship, and her teams were a combined 135–15. Griner was also twice named the nation's No. 1 player. No player ever has combined her agility, size, and speed—keep watching for more great things from this amazing athlete.

Breanna Stewart led with 23 points.

EIGHT IS GREAT

After a women's NCAA tournament that included its share of upsets and exciting wins, the final game was over quickly. And it was won by a team that was used to ending up on top.

The University of Connecticut went on a 19–0 run late in the first half of the championship game against Louisville. They won going away, a 93–60 romp for their eighth NCAA title, tying Tennessee for the most. The Huskies were led by freshman **Breanna Stewart**'s 23 points.

To reach the title game, UConn had to break its Notre Dame jinx. They had lost to the Irish three times in the regular season. In the tournament, they faced them in the national semifinal and won easily, 83–65.

The second-biggest story of this tournament was a huge upset. In the round of 16, Louisville beat Baylor, 82–81. Baylor had won 74 of its previous 75 games, including the 2012 national championship. They had superstar **Brittney Griner** and were expected to romp. The Cardinals played tough defense on Griner, bumping and shoving her all game long. She made no baskets in the first half and ended with only 14 points. And it was her foul with 2.6 seconds left that let Louisville's **Monique Reid** make the game-winning free throws.

Griner was the biggest player in the sport, but Connecticut stood tallest at the end.

FINAL WOMEN'S TOP 10
USA Today Coaches Poll

1. Connecticut
2. Notre Dame
3. Louisville
4. Baylor
5. California
6. Duke
7. Stanford
8. Kentucky
9. Tennessee
10. Georgia

NCAA Champs!

MEN'S DIVISION I

It was an Orange dogpile when Syracuse won in 2003.

2013 **Louisville**	2002 **Maryland**	1991 **Duke**
2012 **Kentucky**	2001 **Duke**	1990 **UNLV**
2011 **Connecticut**	2000 **Michigan State**	1989 **Michigan**
2010 **Duke**	1999 **Connecticut**	1988 **Kansas**
2009 **North Carolina**	1998 **Kentucky**	1987 **Indiana**
2008 **Kansas**	1997 **Arizona**	1986 **Louisville**
2007 **Florida**	1996 **Kentucky**	1985 **Villanova**
2006 **Florida**	1995 **UCLA**	1984 **Georgetown**
2005 **North Carolina**	1994 **Arkansas**	1983 **NC State**
2004 **Connecticut**	1993 **North Carolina**	1982 **North Carolina**
2003 **Syracuse**	1992 **Duke**	1981 **Indiana**
		1980 **Louisville**
		1979 **Michigan State**
		1978 **Kentucky**
		1977 **Marquette**
		1976 **Indiana**
		1975 **UCLA**
		1974 **NC State**
		1973 **UCLA**
		1972 **UCLA**

1971 **UCLA**
1970 **UCLA**
1969 **UCLA**
1968 **UCLA**
1967 **UCLA**
1966 Texas Western
1965 **UCLA**
1964 **UCLA**
1963 Loyola (Illinois)
1962 Cincinnati
1961 Cincinnati
1960 Ohio State
1959 California
1958 Kentucky
1957 North Carolina
1956 San Francisco
1955 San Francisco
1954 La Salle
1953 Indiana
1952 Kansas
1951 Kentucky
1950 City Coll. of N.Y.
1949 Kentucky

1948 **Kentucky**
1947 **Holy Cross**
1946 **Oklahoma A&M**
1945 **Oklahoma A&M**
1944 **Utah**

1943 **Wyoming**
1942 **Stanford**
1941 **Wisconsin**
1940 **Indiana**
1939 **Oregon**

WOMEN'S DIVISION I

2013 **Connecticut**
2012 **Baylor**
2011 **Texas A&M**
2010 **Connecticut**
2009 **Connecticut**
2008 Tennessee
2007 **Tennessee**
2006 Maryland
2005 **Baylor**
2004 **Connecticut**
2003 **Connecticut**
2002 **Connecticut**
2001 **Notre Dame**
2000 **Connecticut**
1999 **Purdue**
1998 Tennessee

1997 **Tennessee**
1996 Tennessee
1995 **Connecticut**
1994 **North Carolina**
1993 **Texas Tech**
1992 Stanford
1991 **Tennessee**
1990 **Stanford**
1989 **Tennessee**
1988 **Louisiana Tech**
1987 **Tennessee**
1986 Texas
1985 **Old Dominion**
1984 USC
1983 **USC**
1982 **Louisiana Tech**

TWO FOR THE TITLE!
Miami Heat stars Dwyane Wade and LeBron James celebrate amid the falling confetti after winning their second straight NBA championship. James holds his Finals MVP trophy, also his second. Read the whole story of their great Finals win over the San Antonio Spurs on page 93.

NBA

NBA 2012-13

The Big Three brought home the big two. The Miami Heat's amazing trio of **LeBron James**, **Dwyane Wade**, and **Chris Bosh** ended up atop the NBA again after the 2012–13 season. But they had to work hard to get there, battling through two tough playoff series (see pages 92-93). One of the biggest reasons—along with the Big Three—for the Heat winning the Southeast Division by a stunning 22 games was its team-record 27-game winning streak. Read more about that on page 94.

Along the road to the Finals, though, the NBA offered up many other great stories outside of Miami.

Perhaps the biggest surprise was the continued growth of the Indiana Pacers. Forward **Paul George** emerged this season as one of the NBA's top all-around players. He led the Pacers to their first conference finals since 2004, and they came within an eyelash of defeating the Heat.

New York City has long been a popular place for basketball. High school and college teams draw big crowds, while the Knicks' home at Madison Square Garden is one of the most famous places to play. In 2012, New York welcomed another team

Paul George

"Wow! This place is phenomenal!"

— CELTICS STAR **KEVIN GARNETT** ON FIRST SEEING THE BROOKLYN NETS HOME, THE BARCLAY CENTER. GARNETT AND FELLOW BOSTON STAR PAUL PIERCE WILL MOVE TO THE NETS IN 2013–14.

as the New Jersey Nets moved to become the Brooklyn Nets. Brooklyn is a borough, or part, of New York City. It's home to millions of people, and they were very excited to have their own team. The team responded by making the playoffs.

Meanwhile, on the West Coast, another city with two teams saw them switch places. For most of the past two decades, the Los Angeles Lakers dominated their town, beating out the L.A. Clippers time and again and winning numerous NBA championships. This year, however, the Clips rose above. They became the hot team in a star-studded town and overshadowed the famous Lakers. Guard **Chris Paul** and forward **Blake Griffin** teamed up to lead the Clippers to the best record in team history and their first division title. A disappointing first-round playoff loss will energize them to keep this rivalry a fierce one.

As always, young players earned a lot of headlines. The best was rookie of the year **Damian Lillard** of the Portland Trail

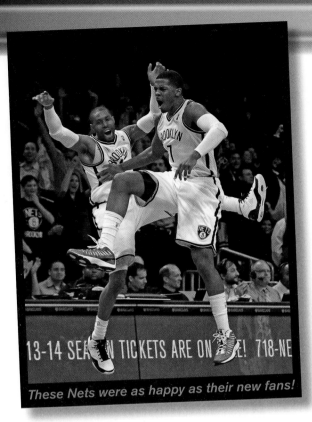

These Nets were as happy as their new fans!

Blazers. He led all rookies in scoring and was rookie of the month in the Western Conference every month! Top draft pick **Anthony Davis** of New Orleans got better and better as the season went along. He had 11 double-doubles (double figures in points and rebounds in one game).

While the young players are the NBA's future, the NBA said goodbye to two veteran All-Stars. Point guard **Jason Kidd** retired after 19 seasons in second place on the NBA's career assists list. He made 10 All-Star Games and led the Nets to two NBA Finals. Small forward **Grant Hill** made seven All-Star Games and was a steady presence for four teams after a championship career at Duke.

The Heat will try for three in a row in the 2013–2014, but look for the Pacers, Clippers, Grizzlies, Thunder, and other up-and-coming teams to try to knock them off. Can King James stay on top?

2012-13 FINAL STANDINGS

EASTERN CONFERENCE

ATLANTIC DIVISION	W–L
Knicks	54–28
Nets	49–33
Celtics	41–40
76ers	34–48
Raptors	34–48

CENTRAL DIVISION	W–L
Pacers	49–32
Bulls	45–37
Bucks	38–44
Pistons	29–53
Cavaliers	24–58

SOUTHEAST DIVISION	W–L
Heat	66–16
Hawks	44–38
Wizards	29–53
Bobcats	21–61
Magic	20–62

WESTERN CONFERENCE

NORTHWEST DIVISION	W–L
Thunder	60–22
Nuggets	57–25
Jazz	43–39
Trail Blazers	33–49
Timberwolves	31–51

SOUTHWEST DIVISION	W–L
Spurs	58–24
Grizzlies	56–26
Rockets	45–37
Mavericks	41–41
Hornets	27–55

PACIFIC DIVISION	W–L
Clippers	56–26
Warriors	47–35
Lakers	45–37
Kings	28–54
Suns	25–57

2013 NBA Playoffs

FIRST ROUND HIGHLIGHTS

➤ Golden State upset No. 3 seed Denver, winning in six games.

➤ A long and rocky Lakers' season ended with a sweep at the hands of the Spurs.

➤ Though the Brooklyn Nets' fans did their best, their team could not find a way to win Game 7 and fell to the Bulls.

The Spurs overwhelmed Randolph and the Grizzlies.

Game 4 of this series needed three overtime periods to come up with a winner. It ended Bulls 142–Nets 134!

➤ The Clippers were one of the Cinderella teams of this 2012-13 season, but they were surprised by the Memphis Grizzlies, who won a first-round surprise in six games. Memphis was down 2–0, but swept the final four games.

SEMIFINALS

➤ The loss of guard **Russell Westbrook** played a big role in the Thunder's loss to the Grizzlies. Memphis star **Zach Randolph** nearly matched scoring star **Kevin Durant** from Oklahoma, but Durant could not win it all by himself.

➤ After squeaking out a double-overtime win to start their series, the San Antonio Spurs won a hard-fought six-game series over Golden State.

➤ Chicago surprised the Heat with a Game 1 win . . . but then Miami rolled, winning one game by 23.

➤ A super season by Indiana continued as they beat the high-scoring New York Knicks to set up a Finals showdown with mighty Miami.

CONFERENCE FINALS

➤ As they had a year earlier, the Miami Heat needed all seven games to earn a trip to the Finals. The upstart Indiana Pacers nearly capped off a dream season, but **LeBron James** & Co. rallied in Game 7 to win the Eastern Conference championship.

➤ Things went more smoothly in the West for another veteran team. The Spurs showed their long playoff experience by sweeping the Grizzlies. Led as usual by **Tim Duncan**, the Spurs handled Memphis easily; only one of the games was as close as five points.

Heat...Repeat
2013 NBA Finals Report

GAME 1
Spurs 92, Heat 88

While **LeBron James** and **Tim Duncan** drew most of the attention, it was shooting guard **Tony Parker** of San Antonio made the biggest shot. It came with 5.2 seconds left and gave the Spurs a surprising win.

GAME 2
Heat 103, Spurs 84

Paying no attention to critics who said the Heat was in trouble, Miami stomped the Spurs in Game 2. **Danny Green's** 5-for-5 on three-pointers helped a lot.

GAME 3
Spurs 113, Heat 77

The surprises continued as the Spurs used the long-range shot to crush the Heat. San Antonio set a Finals record by making 16 three-point shots. Danny Green and **Gary Neal** combined for 13 of those.

GAME 4
Heat 109, Spurs 93

Miami's Big Three showed why they have dominated the NBA. James, **Dwyane Wade**, and **Chris Bosh** combined for 85 points to tie the series. King James led the way with 33 points.

GAME 5
Spurs 114, Heat 104

The Spurs rebounded with a big win. **Manu Ginobili** led the Spurs with 24 points. Green made six more three-pointers.

James split the Spurs D for a key bucket here.

GAME 6
Heat 103, Spurs 100

This was the game the Spurs will remember—and not fondly. Ahead by five with 28 seconds left, the Spurs let the Heat back in. **Ray Allen** hit a game-tying three-point shot to force overtime. In the extra period, the Heat played tough D and made key free throws to snatch the big win. James called it "by far the best game I've ever been a part of."

GAME 7
Heat 95, Spurs 88

No team had won two in a row in this Finals. One team had to win this game, however, and in the end, James and his 37 points were the difference. Miami won its second straight championship.

In The Paint

record 17-game win streak to end 2012. However, they started 2013 with a loss to Denver to end the streak.

◀◀◀ Linsanity on the Move

Though **Jeremy Lin** was the toast of New York City in 2012 after his miraculous apperance and stellar play thrilled the basketball world, he did not remain with the Knicks. A free agent, he signed a big three-year contract with the Houston Rockets. One of the season's big early games came when Houston visted New York . . . and Lin led his new team to a big win over his old team! He scored 22 points as the Rockets won, 109–96.

Two Super Streaks

Two teams put together long winning streaks during the 2012–13 season.

* The Miami Heat's streak was the most impressive. The defending champs reeled off 27 straight wins from January to March. They finally lost to the Bulls, falling six games sort of the Lakers' record streak in 1971–72.

* The Los Angeles Clippers had a December to remember, as they wrapped up a team-

Mavs' Beards

In mid-December, the Dallas Mavericks were struggling. They had lost more games than they had won. To inspire themselves, a few key players vowed not to shave until the team had evened its record. The hairy-faced Mavs finally got to use a razor on April 14, when they reached even. **Dirk Nowitzki**, **O.J. Mayo**, **Vince Carter**, **Chris Kaman**, and other Mavs were quite relieved!

◀◀◀ Three-Point Record

Golden State guard **Stephen Curry** made an NBA-record 272 three-point shots this season. He had three more than previous record-holder Ray Allen, even though Curry tried 53 fewer shots. Curry became the first player in NBA history with 250 "treys" and 500 assists in the same season.

In other three-point news, **Deron Williams** of the Nets set a record with nine three-pointers in the first half of a game in April. In February, the Rockets made 23 of the shots in their win over Golden State, tying the league record.

NBA Draft: Top 10 Picks

NO. TEAM	PLAYER, POSITION, COLLEGE
1. Cavaliers	Anthony Bennett, F, UNLV
2. Magic	Victor Olapido, G, Ohio State
3. Wizards	Otto Porter, F, Georgetown
4. Bobcats	Cody Zeller, C, Indiana
5. Suns	Alex Len, C, Maryland
6. Pelicans*	Nerlens Noel, F, Kentucky
7. Kings	Ben McLemore, G, Kansas
8. Pistons	Kentavious Caldwell-Pope, G, Georgia
9. Timberwolves**	Trey Burke, G, Michigan
10. Trail Blazers	C. J. McCollum, G, Lehigh

* Traded to 76ers; ** Traded to Jazz

NBA Awards

MVP X FOUR!

For the second season in a row and the fourth time in his amazing career, **LeBron James** was named the NBA's Most Valuable Player. King James is now tied for third all-time on the career MVP list (see box).

James led the Heat to their second straight championship and third straight trip to the NBA Finals. He had a dominating regular season, too, leading the Heat on their amazing win streak (see page 94). In February, he became the first player ever to score 30 points and shoot 60 percent or better in six straight games! He was also the NBA Finals MVP award. At only 28 years old, James has his eye on records set by Michael Jordan and others . . . let the debate continue— Is King James the greatest player ever?

Most NBA MVP Awards

6 Kareem Abdul-Jabbar
5 Michael Jordan, Bill Russell
4 Wilt Chamberlain, LeBron James

NBA AWARDS

SIXTH MAN	**J.R. Smith**, Knicks
MOST IMPROVED	**Paul George**, Pacers
TOP DEFENDER	**Marc Gasol**, Grizzlies
ROOKIE OF THE YEAR	**Damian Lillard**, Timberwolves
COMMUNITY ASSIST AWARD	**Dwyane Wade**, Heat
ALL-STAR GAME MVP	**Chris Paul**, Clippers

NBA Stat Leaders

Most NBA stats are ranked "per game" (pg). That is, the numbers here are the average each player had for each game he played.

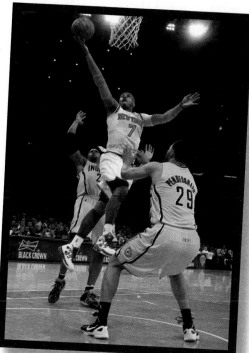

◀◀◀37.1 POINTS PPG
Carmelo Anthony, Knicks

11.1 ASSISTS APG
Rajon Rondo, Celtics

4.1 OFF. REBOUNDS RPG
Zach Randolph, Grizzlies
Tyson Chandler

9.1 DEF. REBOUNDS RPG
Dwight Howard, Lakers

2.4 STEALS SPG
Chris Paul, Clippers

3.0 BLOCKS BPG
Serge Ibaka, Thunder

64.3 FG PCT.
DeAndre Jordan, Clippers

90.5 FT PCT.
Kevin Durant, Thunder

891

The New York Knicks love to dial long distance. In 2012–13, they set this new all-time NBA single-season record for three-point field goals.

2012 WNBA

Parker led the Sparks back to the playoffs.

At the start of the 2012 WNBA season, it looked like the Finals would be a showdown between the defending champion Minnesota Lynx and the hot-starting Connecticut Sun. Both lost only four of their first 19 games and built up big leads in their respective conferences.

The entire WNBA took a break in July so that 12 of its members could represent the U.S. in the Olympics. In all more than 38 current or former WNBA players took part, including players from Australia, Russia, France, Turkey, and Brazil. The WNBA-led U.S. team won the gold.

When the WNBA teams returned to their home courts, the action heated up in both conferences. The Lynx and Sun continued their solid play, but the Los **Angeles Sparks** and Indiana Fever played great basketball, too. The Sparks were looking for their first winning season since 2009, led by All-Star **Candace Parker**. The Fever, behind shooting star Katie Douglas and 2011 MVP **Tamika Catchings**, were giving the Sun a run in the East.

Once the playoffs began, the Fever got hotter. They knocked off the highly-favored Sun to make the Finals. In the West, the Lynx did their job, defeating the surprising Sparks to earn their second straight trip to the Finals. The full report on Indiana's WNBA Finals win is on the opposite page.

Off the court, the WNBA continues to get stronger. Games 3 and 4 of the WNBA Finals (see next page) were huge sellouts. Sponsorships of teams by companies is up, and some playoff games had their highest TV ratings in more than a decade.

2012 AWARDS AND LEADERS

SCORING: **Diana Taurasi**, Phoenix, 21.6 points per game
WNBA MVP: **Tina Charles**, Connecticut
DEFENSIVE PLAYER OF THE YEAR: **Tamika Catchings**, Indiana
SCORING LEADER: **Angel McCoughtry,** Atlanta, 21.3 ppg
REBOUNDS LEADER: **Tina Charles**, Connecticut, 10.5 rpg
ASSISTS LEADER: **Lindsay Whalen**, Minnesota, 5.4 apg

2012 WNBA FINALS

GAME 1 Fever 76, Lynx 70

Indiana was playing on the road against the defending champions, and their leading scorer, Katie Douglas, was on the bench with an injured ankle. But they ignored all that and came out hot, leading by 10 points in the second quarter. They held out against a late Lynx rally to surprise the champs.

GAME 2 Lynx 83, Fever 71

Things got back on track in Game 2, as the Lynx poured on the power in the second half. Seimone Augustus had 23 points after halftime as the defending champs evened the best-of-five series.

GAME 3 Fever 76, Lynx 59

Catchings (22) was a Fever Believer!

The Fever showed that they truly belonged in this series with a dominating Game 3 win. They were up by as much as 70–33, the biggest lead ever in a WNBA Finals game. Indiana's Shavonte Zellous picked a good game to score a career-high 30 points.

2012 WNBA FINAL STANDINGS
REGULAR SEASON

EASTERN CONFERENCE		WESTERN CONFERENCE	
Connecticut	25-9	Minnesota	27-7
Indiana	22-12	Los Angeles	24-10
Atlanta	19-15	San Antonio	21-13
New York	15-19	Seattle	16-18
Chicago	14-20	Tulsa	9-25
Washington	5-29	Phoenix	7-27

GAME 4
Fever 87, Lynx 78

Tamika Catchings has played 12 seasons with the Fever, been an All-Star, and helped the U.S. win Olympic gold. But she had never been a WNBA champ until she led the Fever to this clinching victory on their home court. Catchings scored 25 points and was named the Finals MVP as the Fever became WNBA champs for the first time in their history.

Stat Stuff

NBA CHAMPIONS

2012–13 **Miami**	2008–09 **L.A. Lakers**	1993–94 **Houston**
2011–12 **Miami**	2007–08 **Boston**	1992–93 **Chicago**
2010–11 **Dallas**	2006–07 **San Antonio**	1991–92 **Chicago**
2009–10 **L.A. Lakers**	2005–06 **Miami**	1990–91 **Chicago**
	2004–05 **San Antonio**	1989–90 **Detroit**
	2003–04 **Detroit**	1988–89 **Detroit**
	2002–03 **San Antonio**	1987–88 **L.A. Lakers**
	2001–02 **L.A. Lakers**	1986–87 **L.A. Lakers**
	2000–01 **L.A. Lakers**	1985–86 **Boston**
	1999–00 **L.A. Lakers**	1984–85 **L.A. Lakers**
	1998–99 **San Antonio**	1983–84 **Boston**
	1997–98 **Chicago**	1982–83 **Philadelphia**
	1996–97 **Chicago**	1981–82 **L.A. Lakers**
	1995–96 **Chicago**	1980–81 **Boston**
	1994–95 **Houston**	1979–80 **L.A. Lakers**

Walt Frazier of the 1973 Knicks

1978-79 **Seattle**

1977-78 **Washington**

1976-77 **Portland**

1975-76 **Boston**

1974-75 **Golden State**

1973-74 **Boston**

1972-73 **New York**

1971-72 **L.A. Lakers**

1970-71 **Milwaukee**

1969-70 **New York**

1968-69 **Boston**

1967-68 **Boston**

1966-67 **Philadelphia**

1965-66 **Boston**

1964-65 **Boston**

1963-64 **Boston**

1962-63 **Boston**

1961-62 **Boston**

1960-61 **Boston**

1959-60 **Boston**

1958-59 **Boston**

1957-58 **St. Louis**

1956-57 **Boston**

1955-56 **Philadelphia**

1954-55 **Syracuse**

1953-54 **Minneapolis**

1952-53 **Minneapolis**

1951-52 **Minneapolis**

1950-51 **Rochester**

1949-50 **Minneapolis**

1948-49 **Minneapolis**

1947-48 **Baltimore**

1946-47 **Philadelphia**

WNBA CHAMPIONS

2012 **Indiana**

2011 **Minnesota**

2010 **Seattle**

2009 **Phoenix**

2008 **Detroit**

2007 **Phoenix**

2006 **Detroit**

2005 **Sacramento**

2004 **Seattle**

2003 **Detroit**

2002 **Los Angeles**

2001 **Los Angeles**

2000 **Houston**

1999 **Houston**

1998 **Houston**

1997 **Houston**

NHL

STANLEY'S KIND OF TOWN
Amid flying confetti and the cheers of thousands of fans, Chicago Blackhawks star Patrick Kane hoists the Stanley Cup at a parade in the team's honor. The Blackhawks beat the Bruins in an exciting Stanley Cup Finals for their second championship in four seasons. Read all about it on page 107.

A Mini-Season!

What was supposed to be the 2012–2013 NHL season ended up being just the 2013 season. In Fall 2012, when the season was supposed to start, the players and owners could not agree on a contract. After many meetings, the league cancelled games until they could agree.

No games were played in October, November, or December. More than 500 games and the All-Star Game were cancelled before play finally resumed on January 19, 2013. The mini-season would be 48 games, not the usual 82.

A team that made a fast start would be in good shape in a shorter season. That team was the Chicago Blackhawks. They started by defeating the defending champion Los Angeles Kings and never looked back. The Blackhawks set an NHL record to open a season, going 24 games without a loss. Chicago goalie **Ray Emery** set his own record with 12 straight wins in the nets.

While the Blackhawks bulldozed their way through the Western Conference, the Pittsburgh Penguins made some noise in the East, leading the league in goals scored and eventually challenging the Blackhawks for the best overall record as the season progressed.

Two big guns provided offensive fireworks. Washington Capitals wing **Alex Ovechkin** scored 32 goals and Tampa Bay Lightening center **Steven Stamkos** notched 29 goals in only 48 games. There's no telling what they would have done in a full 82-game season!

As good as Ovechkin and Stamkos were at shooting pucks, Columbus Blue Jackets goalie **Sergei Bobrovsky** was great at stopping them. Bobrovsky played in 37 games and allowed an average of 2.00 goals per game. Incredibly, Bobrovsky did this with a team that finished the regular season in 17th place overall.

Ovechkin was the Caps' goal-scoring machine.

Tavares led the Islanders to the playoffs.

FINAL STANDINGS

EASTERN CONFERENCE	W	L	OT	PTS
1 Pittsburgh	36	12	0	72
2 Montréal	29	14	5	63
3 Washington	27	18	3	57
4 Boston	28	14	6	62
5 Toronto	26	17	5	57
6 NY Rangers	26	18	4	56
7 Ottawa	25	17	6	56
8 NY Islanders	24	17	7	55
9 Winnipeg	24	21	3	51
10 Philadelphia	23	22	3	49
11 New Jersey	19	19	10	48
12 Buffalo	21	21	6	48
13 Carolina	19	25	4	42
14 Tampa Bay	18	26	4	40
15 Florida	15	27	6	36

WESTERN CONFERENCE	W	L	OT	PTS
1 Chicago	36	7	5	77
2 Anaheim	30	12	6	66
3 Vancouver	26	15	7	59
4 St. Louis	29	17	2	60
5 Los Angeles	27	16	5	59
6 San Jose	25	16	7	57
7 Detroit	24	16	8	56
8 Minnesota	26	19	3	55
9 Columbus	24	17	7	55
10 Phoenix	21	18	9	51
11 Dallas	22	22	4	48
12 Edmonton	19	22	7	45
13 Calgary	19	25	4	42
14 Nashville	16	23	9	41
15 Colorado	16	25	7	39

There were also some surprises. The Anaheim Ducks and Montreal Canadiens rebounded from poor 2011–2012 seasons to finish among the league's elite teams. The Toronto Maple Leafs made it to the playoffs after a nine-year drought; while the New York Islanders, led by superstar captain **John Tavares** (who was also a finalist for the league's MVP), made their first playoff appearance since the 2006–2007 season. The Islanders made more headlines when they announced plans to move to Brooklyn's Barclays Center for the 2014–2015 season.

As some teams climbed to the top, others fell shockingly to the bottom. The New Jersey Devils came two games short of winning the 2012 Stanley Cup, but finished 22nd overall in 2012–2013. The news got worse for the Devils when their big-scoring wing, **Ilya Kovalchuk**, announced his retirement in July.

If there was any silver lining in the shortened season, it was the fact that teams were all very close in the standings and competed for playoff spots up to the last regular-season games. That made the playoffs even more intense than usual.

NHL Playoffs

Boston's playoff successes sent them to the Finals.

Close Call

The Blackhawks came within one shot of having their season end early. Detroit took Chicago to seven games, and even led late in Game 7. However, the Blackhawks forced overtime on a **Henrik Zetterberg** goal with 26 seconds left, then won in overtime.

I n the first round, the Blackhawks knocked out the Minnesota Wild in five games, but the Bruins had to battle the Toronto Maple Leafs in a seven-game heart-stopper. In the second round, the Bruins pushed aside the New York Rangers, but the Blackhawks had a tough time with a determined Detroit Red Wings squad.

The Conference Finals usually produce some of the most intense matchups. While the Blackhawks easily defeated the defending-champion Los Angeles Kings, the Bruins took on the heavily favored Pittsburgh Penguins. The Penguins were led by the high scoring of **Sidney Crosby**, **Evgeni Malkin**, and **James Neal**, who had combined for a total of 28 goals in the first two rounds. But the

Bruins got spectacular play from their goalie, Tuukka Rask, and shut out the Penguins 3–0. The Penguins lost their cool, the game, and ultimately the series in an easy sweep for the Bruins. The Penguins managed only two goals in the entire series. Boston and Chicago faced off for the Stanley Cup.

The Tough Get Going

The NHL playoffs are a time when courage stands out. When starting Minnesota Wild goalie **Niklas Backstrom** was injured before the first game of the playoffs, backup **Josh Harding** was rushed into the series. Harding suffers from multiple sclerosis and impressed everyone with his heroism. And Bruins center **Gregory Campbell** played for more than minute with a broken leg after being hit with a puck. Ouch!

PLAY-OFF RESULTS
(Games won in parentheses)

FIRST ROUND

EASTERN CONFERENCE
Pittsburgh OVER NY Islanders (4-2)
Ottawa OVER Montreal (4-1)
NY Rangers OVER Washington (4-3)
Boston OVER Toronto (4-3)

WESTERN CONFERENCE
Chicago OVER Minnesota (4-1)
Detroit OVER Anaheim (4-3)
San Jose OVER Vancouver (4-0)
Los Angeles OVER St. Louis (4-2)

CONFERENCE SEMIFINALS

EASTERN CONFERENCE
Pittsburgh OVER Ottawa (4-1)
Boston OVER NY Rangers (4-1)

WESTERN CONFERENCE
Chicago OVER Detroit (4-3)
Los Angeles OVER San Jose (4-3)

CONFERENCE FINALS

EASTERN CONFERENCE
Boston OVER Pittsburgh (4-0)

WESTERN CONFERENCE
Chicago OVER Los Angeles (4-1)

STANLEY CUP FINALS
Chicago OVER Boston (4-2)

What a Finish!

The final series between the Blackhawks and the Bruins made up for all the disappointment of the shortened season. It was a great battle between two very tough teams. Three of the first four games needed overtime to decide a winner. After five games, Chicago had a 3–2 lead.

An intense Game 6 featured great work by both goalies. Midway through the third period, the Bruins' **Milan Lucic** scored to give his team a 2–1 lead. It looked like the series was heading for a deciding Game 7. One hockey commentator was in an elevator headed to the ice for interviews! But the Blackhawks still had some magic up their sleeves. They tied the game with 1:16 remaining. Then, incredibly, with less than 18 seconds left, Blackhawks center **Dave Bolland** slipped behind the Bruins defense to stuff in the game-winning goal and clinch the Cup. It was one of the most dramatic Cup-winning games ever.

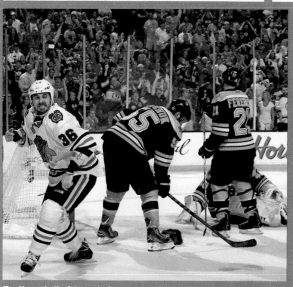

Bolland (left) celebrates after his winning goal!

Ice Time!

Why Did Hockey Stop?

In the 2012-12 season, the NHL cancelled more than 500 games, while fans waited for the season to start. Why?

As usual, it all came down to money. Under the old agreement, the players were guaranteed 57 percent of the money that comes in to the NHL and its teams. The team owners wanted to reduce that to 46 percent.

The problem is that only a few NHL teams actually make money. The rest survive thanks to rules that share money from the league to every team. The players argued that they're the ones who bring in the money. The owners said the players were making enough.

After four months, the two sides agreed. The players took a cut, but a much smaller one than the owners wanted. Future seasons will now start on time! The bottom line for fans? Let's keep dropping the pucks!

A line of Staals: The three brothers (in red) face off for Carolina.

▲ Staal in the Family

The **Staal brothers** are the NHL's current "hockey family," but up until the 2013 season, they all played for different teams. That changed when **Jordan** was traded to **Eric's** Carolina Hurricanes. Later that season, the Hurricanes called up **Jared** Staal from the minors. On April 26, 2013, Jared made his NHL debut, starting on a line with Eric and Jordan! The team they played against was the New York Rangers, for whom their other brother, **Marc**, plays. Unfortunately, Marc was injured at the time.

The "New" NHL

In the offseason, the NHL moved a few things around. Starting in 2013, two teams, the Red Wings and Blue Jackets, moved from the Eastern to Western Conferences. Each conference was re-arranged to have two divisions instead of three. In the East, the NHL has the Atlantic and Metropolitan Divisions. In the West, fans will watch the Central and Pacific Divisions. Check nhl.com to see where your favorite team ended up.

Hard-Nosed Harding

Josh Harding, the backup goaltender for the Minnesota Wild, had just signed a three-year contract extension with the team in July 2012. In November, he was diagnosed with multiple sclerosis. The nerve disease can cause blurred vision and lack of coordination, but Harding was determined to press on with his career. In his first game back, he stopped all 24 shots in a 1-0 victory over the Dallas Stars. He also had to step in for the team's injured starter in the playoffs. For his hard work and courage, Harding won a special postseason award (see page 110).

Super Streak!

The Chicago Blackhawks set an NHL record on February 22, 2013. By defeating the San Jose Sharks, they had gone unbeaten for 17 straight games. The Blackhawks eventually extended their streak to 24 games—going 21-0-3 record before finally losing to the Colorado Avalanche. The Blackhawks were the NHL's best from beginning to end, starting the season with the record-breaking points streak and ending it by hoisting the Stanley Cup.

World Junior Champs

For international hockey fans, only the Olympics is a bigger event than the World Junior Hockey Championships. In the 2013 semifinals, the United States routed Canada, 5-1. In the gold-medal game against Sweden, Team USA's **Rocco Grimaldi** scored a pair of goals. In a bit of an upset, the U.S. won 3–1, and goaltender **John Gibson** was named tournament MVP. Team USA included players from Pennsylvania, California, Florida, Illinois, Michigan, Ohio, Texas, and Wisconsin—a mark of how ice hockey is growing in popularity.

Captain Jake McCabe

2012-13 Awards

Bobrovsky was the first Russian to win the coveted Vezina Trophy.

This award means a lot, to be recognized by the guys that you compete against each and every night.

— PITTSBURGH STAR SIDNEY CROSBY ON WINNING HIS SECOND LINDSAY AWARD

Conn Smythe Trophy
(Stanley Cup Playoffs MVP)
PATRICK KANE, Chicago Blackhawks

President's Trophy
(Best Regular-Season Record)
CHICAGO BLACKHAWKS

Hart Trophy (MVP)
ALEX OVECHKIN, Washington Capitals

Ted Lindsay Award
(Outstanding Player as Voted by the Players)
SIDNEY CROSBY, Pittsburgh Penguins

Vezina Trophy (Best Goaltender)
SERGEI BOBROVSKY,
Columbus Blue Jackets

James Norris Memorial Trophy
(Best Defenseman)
P.K. SUBBAN, Montreal Canadiens

Calder Memorial Trophy (Best Rookie)
JONATHAN HUBERDEAU,
Florida Panthers

Frank J. Selke Trophy
(Best Defensive Forward)
JONATHAN TOEWS,
Chicago Blackhawks

Lady Byng Memorial Trophy
(Most Gentlemanly Player)
MARTIN ST. LOUIS,
Tampa Bay Lightning

Jack Adams Award (Best Coach)
PAUL MACLEAN, Ottawa Senators

Bill Masterson Memorial Trophy
(Perseverance and Dedication to the Game)
JOSH HARDING, Minnesota Wild

2012-13 Stat Leaders

60 POINTS ▶▶▶
Martin St. Louis, Lightning

32 GOALS
Alex Ovechkin, Capitals

43 ASSISTS
Martin St. Louis, Lightning

1.69 GOALS AGAINST AVG.
Craig Anderson, Senators

.941 SAVE PERCENTAGE
Craig Anderson, Senators)

5 SHUTOUTS
Five players tied

24 WINS/GOALIE
Henrik Lundqvist, Rangers;
Antti Niemi, Sharks;
Niklas Backstrom, Wild

+31 PLUS/MINUS
Pascal Dupuis, Penguins

644 FACEOFFS
Claude Giroux, Flyers

669

That's the all-time career record for wins by a goalie held by **Martin Brodeur** of the Devils. In his 20th NHL season, he had 13 wins in 2013 to reach that total. And he's expected to be back for more next season.

Stanley Cup Champions

Season	Champion		Season	Champion
2012-13	Chicago Blackhawks		1986–87	Edmonton Oilers
2011–12	Los Angeles Kings		1985–86	Montreal Canadiens
2010–11	Boston Bruins		1984–85	Edmonton Oilers
2009–10	Chicago Blackhawks		1983–84	Edmonton Oilers
2008–09	Pittsburgh Penguins		1982–83	New York Islanders
2007–08	Detroit Red Wings		1981–82	New York Islanders
2006–07	Anaheim Ducks		1980–81	New York Islanders
2005–06	Carolina Hurricanes		1979–80	New York Islanders
2004–05	No champion (Lockout)		1978–79	Montreal Canadiens
2003–04	Tampa Bay Lightning		1977–78	Montreal Canadiens
2002–03	New Jersey Devils		1976–77	Montreal Canadiens
2001–02	Detroit Red Wings		1975–76	Montreal Canadiens
2000–01	Colorado Avalanche		1974–75	Philadelphia Flyers
1999–00	New Jersey Devils		1973–74	Philadelphia Flyers
1998–99	Dallas Stars		1972–73	Montreal Canadiens
1997–98	Detroit Red Wings		1971–72	Boston Bruins
1996–97	Detroit Red Wings		1970–71	Montreal Canadiens
1995–96	Colorado Avalanche		1969–70	Boston Bruins
1994–95	New Jersey Devils		1968–69	Montreal Canadiens
1993–94	New York Rangers		1967–68	Montreal Canadiens
1992–93	Montreal Canadiens		1966–67	Toronto Maple Leafs
1991–92	Pittsburgh Penguins		1965–66	Montreal Canadiens
1990–91	Pittsburgh Penguins		1964–65	Montreal Canadiens
1989–90	Edmonton Oilers		1963–64	Toronto Maple Leafs
1988–89	Calgary Flames		1962–63	Toronto Maple Leafs
1987–88	Edmonton Oilers		1961–62	Toronto Maple Leafs

1960–61	**Chicago Blackhawks**
1959–60	**Montreal Canadiens**
1958–59	**Montreal Canadiens**
1957–58	**Montreal Canadiens**
1956–57	**Montreal Canadiens**
1955–56	**Montreal Canadiens**
1954–55	**Detroit Red Wings**
1953–54	**Detroit Red Wings**
1952–53	**Montreal Canadiens**
1951–52	**Detroit Red Wings**
1950–51	**Toronto Maple Leafs**
1949–50	**Detroit Red Wings**
1948–49	**Toronto Maple Leafs**
1947–48	**Toronto Maple Leafs**
1946–47	**Toronto Maple Leafs**
1945–46	**Montreal Canadiens**
1944–45	**Toronto Maple Leafs**
1943–44	**Montreal Canadiens**
1942–43	**Detroit Red Wings**
1941–42	**Toronto Maple Leafs**
1940–41	**Boston Bruins**
1939–40	**New York Rangers**
1938–39	**Boston Bruins**
1937–38	**Chicago Blackhawks**
1936–37	**Detroit Red Wings**
1935–36	**Detroit Red Wings**
1934–35	**Montreal Maroons**
1933–34	**Chicago Blackhawks**
1932–33	**New York Rangers**

MOST STANLEY CUP TITLES

Montreal Canadiens	**23**
Toronto Maple Leafs	**13**
Detroit Red Wings	**11**
Boston Bruins	**6**
Edmonton Oilers	**5**

1931–32	**Toronto Maple Leafs**
1930–31	**Montreal Canadiens**
1929–30	**Montreal Canadiens**
1928–29	**Boston Bruins**
1927–28	**New York Rangers**
1926–27	**Ottawa Senators**
1925–26	**Montreal Maroons**
1924–25	**Victoria Cougars**
1923–24	**Montreal Canadiens**
1922–23	**Ottawa Senators**
1921–22	**Toronto St. Pats**
1920–21	**Ottawa Senators**
1919–20	**Ottawa Senators**
1918–19	No decision
1917–18	**Toronto Arenas**

NASCAR

A NEW CHAMPION!
After holding off five-time champ Jimmie Johnson, Brad Keselowski got to wave the flag and spin his tires to celebrate winning his first NASCAR Sprint Cup championship in 2012.

Big W for Brad K.!

Heading into the 2013 Chase for the Sprint Cup, it looked like **Jimmie Johnson** would grab championship No. 6. He had always done well on the Chase tracks, and he started this season's final 10-race stretch only three points behind leader **Denny Hamlin**. However, he was part of a tight pack, and after the first few weeks, a new leader emerged. **Brad Keselowski** won the first and third races of the Chase . . . and the Chase was on.

Keselowski was not exactly an unknown as the Chase season heated up. He had made headlines several times during the 2012 season, though not always in a good way. He won three races—at Pocono, Talladega, and Kentucky. But he also was fined for tweeting while in his car. He was stopped at the time, waiting for the track to clear at Daytona, but NASCAR officials didn't like it. They changed their minds later in the summer when they saw how many fans were following the outspoken young driver.

After Keselowski took over the Chase lead by winning at Dover, he still had work to do to hold off a field of top drivers. Three races from the end of the year, he actually

No. 2 was No. 1: Keselowski and Johnson (48 at left) raced to the finish in 2012.

CHASE FOR THE CUP

2012 FINAL STANDINGS

1 **Brad KESELOWSKI**
2 **Clint BOWYER**
3 **Jimmie JOHNSON**
4 **Kasey KAHNE**
5 **Greg BIFFLE**
6 **Denny HAMLIN**
7 **Matt KENSETH**
8 **Kevin HARVICK**
9 **Tony STEWART**
10 **Jeff GORDON**
11 **Martin TRUEX Jr.**
12 **Dale EARNHARDT Jr.**

"These guys [on my team] make me fast enough and strong enough. I can't be here without them. I really can't. This isn't a one-man effort. I might get the glory, but it's about these guys, it's about my family."

—2012 NASCAR Champ BRAD KESELOWSKI

lost the lead to Johnson. In a dramatic showdown in Texas, the pair raced side by side near the end. A final green-white-checkered finish provided drama for fans and drivers alike. Johnson surged ahead at the last moment to hold off his hard-charging rival.

"I raced hard," Keselowski said afterward. "It was just a dogfight."

With Johnson now clinging to a seven-point lead, the dogfights kept coming over the final two races. At Phoenix the next week, Keselowski finished sixth, while Johnson plummeted to 31st.

The final race of the season was as dramatic as anything fans had seen all year. The race was in Miami. Johnson needed to finish 20 points ahead of his rival, while Keselowski wanted just to stay near to Johnson throughout the race so he could hold his Chase lead.

Johnson knew the situation he was in. "Well, if we're racing each other I'm in trouble. We need a big gap between where

I am and where he is. That's really the bottom line."

However, the veteran five-time champ got that gap early in the race, zooming ahead of Keselowski. However, a problem with a tire caused Johnson to have to return to the pit mid-race. Then, an engine problem ended his day early. Meanwhile, Keselowski drove safely but swiftly, avoiding trouble. With 24 laps remaining, Keselowski got the news on his radio that his team had clinched the championship.

Along with the driver winning his first, it was the first for a guy who has done a lot of winning everywhere else. Team owner **Roger Penske** first earned fame in Indy cars. His drivers have won a record 15 Indianapolis 500s and 12 Indy Racing League titles. However, this was the first time that the well-liked, veteran owner led a NASCAR champ.

Now that's news to tweet about.

$6.2

That's how many dollars—in millions!—that **Brad Keselowski** drove home after winning his first NASCAR championship.

Around the Track: 2012

▲ Earnhardt's Luck

The 2012 season had some high points for popular driver **Dale Earnhardt Jr.** He won the Michigan 400 for his first victory in several seasons. And he had enough high finishes to earn a spot in the season-ending Chase for the Cup. However, that's where his season went backward. In the October event at Talladega Motor Speedway, Earnhardt was part of a huge wreck. More than 25 cars were involved in one way or another on the final lap. Earnhardt hit the wall so hard he got a concussion. Doctors told him he had to miss the next two races to recover. It was good news that he would come back, but bad news that he would miss races. With only 10 events on the Chase schedule, the missed races cost Earnhardt a shot at the title.

Off-Track Battles

NASCAR drivers go nose-to-tail and bumper-to-bumper every weekend. The action usually stops once they stop the cars, however. Late in the race at Phoenix, **Jeff Gordon** and **Clint Bowyer** tangled on the track. Bowyer clipped Gordon and sent him into the wall. A lap later, Gordon swiped Bowyer and wrecked both cars. After the cars returned to the pit area, Bowyer got nose-to-nose with Gordon, angry at the wreck. Gordon stood his ground, and the two teams nearly came to blows. Both drivers were fined points and money for their off-track actions.

NASCAR Hall of Fame

Meet the 2013 Inductees!

Buck Baker, DRIVER
First to win back-to-back NASCAR titles (1956–57); won 46 races

Cotton Owens, DRIVER/OWNER
After a racing career, became car owner and won 1966 title with David Pearson.

Herb Thomas, DRIVER
First to win two NASCAR titles (1951 and 1953); finished second three other times

Rusty Wallace, DRIVER
Won 55 races; 1989 NASCAR champion; from racing family (father and two brothers); now a TV commentator

Leonard Wood, CREW CHIEF
Ran the pits and mechanics for the family's NASCAR racing teams in the 1960; innovative engine maker and fix-it man

NATIONWIDE SERIES

The 2012 NASCAR Nationwide Series season started with a bang, as **Danica Patrick** won the pole at the first race. It was the former Indy star's first full season in stock cars. She ended up 10th overall in points before making the leap to Sprint Cup in 2013. **Ricky Stenhouse Jr.** *(left)*, the defending Nationwide champ, won three of the season's first 10 races to build a solid points lead. In July, at the first Nationwide race at the famed Indianapolis Motor Speedway, eventual Sprint Cup champ **Brad Keselowski** dipped down a class to win. Another Sprint Cup driver, young **Joey Logano**, won three of the final six races. In the end, the result was the same as the previous season. Stenhouse finished like he started, winning three of the final 10 races to clinch his second straight Nationwide series title.

TRUCK SERIES

In the NASCAR Camping World Truck Series, young **James Buescher** was the first driver of the season to win a second race. In fact, he won three of the first 10 races of the season and was the driver to beat as the summer wore on. At a key race in Kentucky in September, Buescher won his fourth race. Those points would prove crucial as he struggled down the stretch, not finishing above sixth in the final four races. Meanwhile, **Joey Coulter** had a trio of thirds in the same stretch, while **Timothy Peters** had good finishes. In the end, Buescher had six more points than Peters and won his first Truck Series championship.

Buescher (No. 31) held off all his rivals for his first title.

Daytona Double

Five-time NASCAR champion Jimmie Johnson started off the 2013 season with a bang, winning his second Daytona 500. But the drivers returned to Daytona in July for the Coke Zero 400 . . . and Johnson won again! He was the first driver since 1982 to sweep the season's races at the famed track in Florida.

Talladega Had One, Too!

The big, wide racetrack at Talladega in Alabama often leads to multi-car crashes. In the May 2013 race there, it was business as usual. A 16-car wreck took out many top names, while an 11-car wreck forced the field into a green-white-checkered sprint to the finish. The race was also halted due to a huge rainstorm. After waiting hours, the final sprint was held, and eight-year vet **David Ragan** won his second career race.

DANICA'S BIG SPLASH!

Danica Patrick (10), the former Indy star turned NASCAR rookie, showed that she could race with the big boys. In February, 2013, she won the pole position at the fabled Daytona 500. Not only was she the first woman to do that, she was the first female driver to win the pole in any NASCAR race . . . and they've been drivin' 'round the tracks since 1949! She finished the race in eighth place.

GEN-6 CARS
REPORT

The Car of Tomorrow is for yesterday. The single-design cars that NASCAR Sprint Cup teams had used for the past several years were replaced in 2013. The new Gen-6 car, as it's known, is the standard for all teams going forward. The Gen-6 design returns to the series' stock-car roots. The race cars now mirror street cars. From the nose to the side panels, the cars look like a Ford Fusion or a Toyota Camry or other cars. They move a lot faster than your family's Camry, of course!

Safety was a big part of the Gen-6 design. The driver's cockpit protects them from almost any kind of crash.

Because all but two races are run on tracks with left turns only, the cars are designed to be different on the side closest to the inside of the track. The rear fin is angled that way, the right side is flatter to create better airflow, and the left side is 60 pounds lighter.

All the changes have helped make the action on the track better. Through June, races were closer than they had been, on average, in 10 years. More cars were finishing races, too.

That Man Again

Jimmie Johnson won five NASCAR championships in a row (2006–2010) but saw other drivers earn the top spot in 2011 and 2012. However, as 2013 roared on, he looked like he was out to capture No. 6. He won at Daytona, tiny Martinsville, and the 1.5-mile track at Pocono, New York. Big tracks or small, Johnson can win anywhere. All those Ws gave him a strong lead heading toward the Chase season. So, for our official prediction, we proclaim:

★ 2013 NASCAR CHAMP: **Jimmie Johnson** ★

NASCAR Champions

Year	Champion	Make		Year	Champion	Make
2012	Brad Keselowski	Ford		1993	Dale Earnhardt Sr.	Chevrolet
2011	Tony Stewart	Chevrolet		1992	Alan Kulwicki	Ford
2010	Jimmie Johnson	Chevrolet		1991	Dale Earnhardt Sr.	Chevrolet
2009	Jimmie Johnson	Chevrolet		1990	Dale Earnhardt Sr.	Chevrolet
2008	Jimmie Johnson	Chevrolet		1989	Rusty Wallace	Pontiac
2007	Jimmie Johnson	Chevrolet		1988	Bill Elliott	Ford
2006	Jimmie Johnson	Chevrolet		1987	Dale Earnhardt Sr.	Chevrolet
2005	Tony Stewart	Chevrolet		1986	Dale Earnhardt Sr.	Chevrolet
2004	Kurt Busch	Ford		1985	Darrell Waltrip	Chevrolet
2003	Matt Kenseth	Ford		1984	Terry Labonte	Chevrolet
2002	Tony Stewart	Pontiac		1983	Bobby Allison	Buick
2001	Jeff Gordon	Chevrolet		1982	Darrell Waltrip	Buick
2000	Bobby Labonte	Pontiac		1981	Darrell Waltrip	Buick
1999	Dale Jarrett	Ford		1980	Dale Earnhardt Sr.	Chevrolet
1998	Jeff Gordon	Chevrolet		1979	Richard Petty	Chevrolet
1997	Jeff Gordon	Chevrolet		1978	Cale Yarborough	Oldsmobile
1996	Terry Labonte	Chevrolet		1977	Cale Yarborough	Chevrolet
1995	Jeff Gordon	Chevrolet		1976	Cale Yarborough	Chevrolet
1994	Dale Earnhardt Sr.	Chevrolet		1975	Richard Petty	Dodge

Year	Driver	Make		Year	Driver	Make
1974	Richard Petty	Dodge		1961	Ned Jarrett	Chevrolet
1973	Benny Parsons	Chevrolet		1960	Rex White	Chevrolet
1972	Richard Petty	Plymouth		1959	Lee Petty	Plymouth
1971	Richard Petty	Plymouth		1958	Lee Petty	Oldsmobile
1970	Bobby Isaac	Dodge		1957	Buck Baker	Chevrolet
1969	David Pearson	Ford		1956	Buck Baker	Chrysler
1968	David Pearson	Ford		1955	Tim Flock	Chrysler
1967	Richard Petty	Plymouth		1954	Lee Petty	Chrysler
1966	David Pearson	Dodge		1953	Herb Thomas	Hudson
1965	Ned Jarrett	Ford		1952	Tim Flock	Hudson
1964	Richard Petty	Plymouth		1951	Herb Thomas	Hudson
1963	Joe Weatherly	Pontiac		1950	Bill Rexford	Oldsmobile
1962	Joe Weatherly	Pontiac		1949	Red Byron	Oldsmobile

NASCAR'S WINNINGEST DRIVERS
(career Cup series victories entering 2013)

DRIVER	RACES WON		DRIVER	RACES WON
1. Richard PETTY	200		6. Cale YARBOROUGH	83
2. David PEARSON	105		7. Dale EARNHARDT Sr.	76
3. Jeff GORDON	87		8. Jimmie JOHNSON	60
4. Bobby ALLISON	84		9. Rusty WALLACE	55
Darrell WALTRIP	84		10. Lee PETTY	54

OTHER MOTOR SPORTS

IT'S ABOUT TIME!
Tony Kanaan (11) finally captured a prize he's been seeking for more than a decade—a victory at the fabled Indianapolis 500. Read more about the popular Brazilian's big win, and all about IndyCar racing, starting on page 128.

Formula 1

F ormula 1 had a winning formula indeed in 2012. The world-spanning, open-wheel series included 20 races, the most ever in the 63-year history of the sport. Also, fans saw some one of the best fields of drivers, with six former champions taking to the track during the season. From among that field of veterans, however, came the youngest three-time F1 champ ever.

After a nail-biting final race in Brazil, Germany's **Sebastian Vettel** earned his third straight world driving championship. That matched only the great **Juan Manuel Fangio** and Vettel's fellow German star **Michael Schumacher** as winners of three straight. Schumacher, in fact, retired after 2012's final race, capping off one of the greatest careers in motor sports.

2011 F1 FINAL STANDINGS

PLACE/DRIVER	POINTS
1. Sebastian Vettel	392
2. Fernando Alonso	178
3. Kimi Raikkonen	207
4. Lewis Hamilton	190
5. Jenson Button	188

The 2012 season started with a wide-open first half. In the first seven races, seven different drivers won! That was the first time that had happened. **Fernando Alonso** of Spain was the first driver to earn a second victory. Those two wins joined his other high finishes to lead the series most of the summer. Vettel kept chipping away, however. In the 14th race, in Singapore, Vettel found his groove. He won that race and then the next three to move solidly into the lead. However, Alonso kept up the pace and Vettel's lead was only 16 points entering the final race.

In Brazil, Vettel's drive for three almost ended early with a crash in the first lap. However, he and his pit crew got him back on the track. Charging from the back, he made it all the way to sixth place. It wasn't a win, but it was enough to give him the championship by only three points over a disappointed Alonso. It was one of the closest finishes in F1 history.

With help from his crew, Vettel roared back onto the track.

Meet the Champ

Sebastian Vettel has been a pro racer since he was 13. At first, he raced karts, a type of low-slung, high-speed, short-track vehicle. He moved to the senior ranks of karting when he was 15 and joined the Formula BMW Series in 2004, when he was only 17. He won that series title, too. After his talent caught the eye of Formula 1 team owners, and he joined the "big boys" when he was just 19. At a 2007 race in the U.S., he finished eighth and became the youngest driver ever to gain a point in an F1 race.

Of course, he wasn't finished. In 2010, he was second overall in Formula 1 and then won the first of his three titles in 2011.

German star **Michael Schumacher** is considered the greatest Formula 1 driver of all time. Can Vettel challenge his countryman's record of seven championships in a row? With a huge lead already half-way through 2013, Vettel remains the man to beat in Formula 1.

WELCOME BACK TO THE STATES!

For the first time since 2007, Formula 1 racing returned to the United States in 2012. A new track near Austin, Texas, called the Circuit of the Americas was the site. American F1 fans were thrilled to see their favorite type of racing back in the States, but they were still waiting for an American driver to emerge as a contender. In 2012, for example, no American drivers earned a point in an F1 race.

In Austin, however, the race went on, packed with international stars. At the end, it was Britain's **Lewis Hamilton** who took the checkered flag. Hamilton must like racing Stateside . . . he also won the last F1 race held in the U.S.!

Indy Car

Will Power's bad luck was good luck for champ Ryan Hunter-Reay.

Will Power might have one of the coolest names in auto racing, but he has some of the worst luck. In each of the past three IZOD IndyCar seasons, Power has had a chance to win the overall title entering the final race. All three times, he has failed to grab the brass ring.

In 2012, he was 17 points ahead of **Ryan Hunter-Reay** heading into the final event, the MAVTV 500 at Fontana, Calif. But Power's bad luck continued when he smacked into a wall on the 55th lap. Hunter-Reay still had work to do, however. He stayed near the leaders for the rest of the race, even as Power tried to get back into it. In fact, Power had taken off his racing suit before his team managed to fix his car enough for him to drive it again.

However, even their efforts couldn't change the outcome. Hunter-Reay, a Florida native, won his first series title and the first by an American since 2006, when

Sam Hornish Jr. was the champ.

For Power, it was another in a series of tough breaks. "It's depressing to lose the championship again that way," he said after the race. "It's the season [on the line], you can't make mistakes like that."

For his part, Hunter-Reay was elated. "It hasn't sunk in yet. I just drove 500 miles like it was for my life. I can't believe we are INDYCAR champions."

Power had gotten the season off to fast start, winning three of the first four races. However, he didn't win again all season. When Hunter-Reay reeled off consecutive wins in Milwaukee, Iowa, and Toronto, he moved near the overall lead. But this is racing, so it was neck-and-neck to the finish. Along with Hunter-Reay, fellow Brit **Scott Dixon** was on Power's heels. Brazilian star **Helio Castroneves** was also in the hunt.

2012 IZOD INDYCAR SERIES FINAL STANDINGS

PLACE/DRIVER	POINTS
1. Ryan Hunter-Reay	468
2. Will Power	465
3. Scott Dixon	435
4. Helio Castroneves	431
5. Simon Pagenaud	387

OTHER INDYCAR HIGHLIGHTS:

* French driver **Simon Pagenaud** was the 2012 Rookie of the Year after ending the year a surprising fifth overall, helped by five top-five finishes.

* The IndyCar Series returned to Detroit, Michigan, for a race for the first time since 2008. Detroit is the home of several major automakers, so it was fitting that the oldest type of American racing zoom through the Motor City.

* Canadian driver **James Hinchcliffe** won the opening race in Florida in 2013, his first in an IndyCar. Then he topped himself by winning the season's fourth race in Brazil.

◀◀◀ * In April 2013, **Takuma Sato** became the first driver from Japan to win an IndyCar race. He captured the Long Beach Grand Prix.

2013 INDY 500

Every IndyCar driver wants to win the Indy 500, the sport's ultimate prize. But if a driver can't finish first, then most of them would agree that having **Tony Kanaan** win the 2013 Indy 500 comes a pretty close second. The Brazilian driver finally won the big race in his 12th try at the age of 38. One of the most popular drivers on the circuit, he was beaming after sliding across the finish line on what looked like a parade lap. A crash two laps from the end brought out the yellow caution flag. That means no one can pass until the wreck is cleared. Kanaan was out in front at that point, so he enjoyed the cheers of nearly 200,000 fans as he rolled slowly around the massive Indianapolis Speedway. "Life is funny," Kanaan said afterward. "The yellow is my best friend."

SAFETY AND SPEED!

The 2012 IndyCar season was the first in which teams all used the same basic shell, which is the area where the driver sits. To make the cars safer for drivers and more economical for teams, IndyCar started the ICONIC project in 2010. After two years of testing and practice, the new bodies, made by Dallara of Indiana, hit the track. Each racing team gets its own engines, which have to follow strict rules, too. With the gear so closely matched, however, a team's success is more in the hands of drivers than ever.

Motocross/Supercross

2012 AMA Motocross

Motocross is a teeth-rattling, hard-charging racing sport that takes guts and perfect timing. And while one former champ got out early in the season, another hung on for the lead at the end . . . when it counted.

The biggest news of the early season was the return of **James "Bubba" Stewart Jr.**, who had spent most of the previous seasons concentrating on indoor Supercross. He showed he still remembered how to conquer the outdoor tracks by winning the first four races of the season.

But Stewart battled an arm injury in the middle of the season and **Ryan Dungey** (right) took advantage. He grabbed the overall lead and held on through the difficult late-season races. An amazing pit stop during a race in Masschusetts helped him grab valuable points. Motocross riders almost never have time for such stops, but it paid off for Dungey. A week later in upstate New York, Dungey won the race and clinched the season points championship. He went on to win two more races while wearing the coveted No. 1 on his motorcycle.

2013 AMA Supercross

Ryan Villopoto (left) was unable to defending his 2012 Motocross title due to a knee injury. So he made up for that by winning in the indoor Supercross season in 2013! He was absolutely dominant, winning ten of the 17 races in the season. The last one came in the season's final contest in Las Vegas.

"This is a great way to cap the season off," said Villopoto. "We rebounded this year from a bad start at the season opener and won the title. There is no better way to end a season than like this."

Villopoto wasn't kidding about the bad start. At that season-opening race in Anaheim, he earned only five points after finishing 16th. But he rebounded by winning three of the next six races and adding a five-race win streak that started in St. Louis.

2012 NHRA

It's not often that drag racing makes national auto racing history, but that's just what happened in 2012. In the Top Fuel division, **Antron Brown** became the first African American to win a national car racing title. His rival Tony Schumacher didn't make it easy. In the final race of the U.S. Auto Club Finals, Schumacher lost to **Brandon Bernstein** by eight-tenths of a second. That was enough to give Brown the season championship by a slim seven points.

Brown has been racing for 15 years, and this was his sixth season in Top Fuel. "If I can be an inspiration for any of the kids out there who have dreams, any Americans, that's all I want," said Brown after the race. He won six races on the season to build his lead heading into the Finals.

The Funny Car category made its own kind of history. Veteran driver **Jack Beckman** claimed his first season title by only two points over **Ron Capps**.

It was one of the closest finishes in the long history of Funny Car racing. For Beckman, it was a double victory—he had battled back from cancer to claim the title.

In the Pro Stock division, **Allen Johnson** left little doubt about who was the fastest. He won seven races on the season and capped it off with a win at the Finals. It was Johnson's first championship, and it was a family affair. His father builds all the engines for the powerful cars Johnson drives.

In Pro Stock Motorcycles, defending champ **Eddie Krawiec** returned to the top.

Brown rocketed into racing history with a Top Fuel championship.

Major Champions
OF THE 2000s

TOP FUEL DRAGSTERS

YEAR	DRIVER
2012	**Antron Brown**
2011	**Del Worsham**
2010	**Larry Dixon**
2009	**Tony Schumacher**
2008	**Tony Schumacher**
2007	**Tony Schumacher**
2006	**Tony Schumacher**
2005	**Tony Schumacher**
2004	**Tony Schumacher**
2003	**Larry Dixon**
2002	**Larry Dixon**
2001	**Kenny Bernstein**

FUNNY CARS

YEAR	DRIVER
2012	**Jack Beckham**
2011	**Matt Hagan**
2010	**John Force**
2009	**Robert Hight**
2008	**Cruz Pedregon**
2007	**Tony Pedregon**
2006	**John Force**
2005	**Gary Scelzi**
2004	**John Force**
2003	**Tony Pedregon**
2002	**John Force**
2001	**John Force**

PRO STOCK CARS

YEAR	DRIVER
2012	**Allen Johnson**
2011	**Jason Line**
2010	**Greg Anderson**
2009	**Mike Edwards**
2008	**Jeg Coughlin Jr.**
2007	**Jeg Coughlin Jr.**
2006	**Jason Line**
2005	**Greg Anderson**
2004	**Greg Anderson**
2003	**Greg Anderson**
2002	**Jeg Coughlin Jr.**
2001	**Warren Johnson**

FORMULA ONE

YEAR	DRIVER
2012	**Sebastian Vettel**
2011	**Sebastian Vettel**
2010	**Sebastian Vettel**
2009	**Jenson Button**
2008	**Lewis Hamilton**
2007	**Kimi Räikkönen**
2006	**Fernando Alonso**
2005	**Fernando Alonso**
2004	**Michael Schumacher**
2003	**Michael Schumacher**
2002	**Michael Schumacher**
2001	**Michael Schumacher**

INDYCAR SERIES

YEAR	DRIVER
2012	**Ryan Hunter-Reay**
2011	**Dario Franchitti**
2010	**Dario Franchitti**
2009	**Dario Franchitti**
2008	**Scott Dixon**
2007	**Dario Franchitti**
2006	**Sam Hornish Jr. and Dan Wheldon (tie)**
2005	**Dan Wheldon**
2004	**Tony Kanaan**
2003	**Scott Dixon**
2002	**Sam Hornish Jr.**
2001	**Sam Hornish Jr.**

AMA SUPERCROSS

YEAR	DRIVER
2013	**Ryan Villopoto**
2012	**Ryan Dungey**
2011	**Ryan Villopoto**
2010	**Ryan Dungey**
2009	**James Stewart Jr.**
2008	**Chad Reed**
2007	**James Stewart Jr.**
2006	**Ricky Carmichael**
2005	**Ricky Carmichael**
2004	**Chad Reed**
2003	**Ricky Carmichael**
2002	**Ricky Carmichael**
2001	**Ricky Carmichael**

AMA MOTOCROSS

YEAR	RIDER (MOTOCROSS)	RIDER (LITES)
2012	**Ryan Dungey**	**Blake Baggett**
2011	**Ryan Villopoto**	**Dean Wilson**
2010	**Ryan Dungey**	**Trey Canard**
2009	**Chad Reed**	**Ryan Dungey**
2008	**James Stewart Jr.**	**Ryan Villopoto**
2007	**Grant Langston**	**Ryan Villopoto**
2006	**Ricky Carmichael**	**Ryan Villopoto**
2005	**Ricky Carmichael**	**Ivan Tedesco**
2004	**Ricky Carmichael**	**James Stewart Jr.**
2003	**Ricky Carmichael**	**Grant Langston**
2002	**Ricky Carmichael**	**James Stewart Jr.**
2001	**Ricky Carmichael**	**Mike Brown**

ACTION SPORTS

HIGH-FLYING HAWK

Skateboard legend Tony Hawk doesn't take home X Games medals anymore, but he can still show the kids a trick or two. Here, he's flying high above the skateboard vert ramp during the X Games visit to beautiful Barcelona, Spain.

Summer X Games

In 2013, the X Games traveled the world! Events were held in six cities. Here's a report on the Summer Games; see page 138 for the Winter events.

Foz de Iguaçu, Brazil

* A trio of hometown heroes took gold in skateboard events. Brazilians **Bob Burnquist** (Big Air), **Pedro Barros** (Park), and **Leticia Bufoni** (Street) all took home gold medals.

* With all eyes on young stars like **Mitchie Brusco** and **Tom Schaar**, veteran **Bucky Lasek** won the popular Skateboard Vert event. It was his first title in the event in nine years.

* **Scott Speed** has an awesome name for a racer. He had experience in NASCAR and Formula 1, but had never driven on dirt before. In Brazil, he joined RallyCross and ended up winning the event in his first try!

* Australian BMX rider **Kyle Baldock** won a pair of golds in the Park and Dirt events. They were his first medals of any kind at an X Games.

Barcelona, Spain

* **Mitchie Brusco** landed the first-ever 1080 in a Skateboard Vert competition, but his amazing trick wasn't enough for gold. For the second event in a row, Bucky Lasek was the surprise winner.

Kyle Baldock, a guy from Down Under, went up high to win the BMX Park event.

Brazil's Leticia Bufoni won gold at home.

* **Laia Sanz** won her first X Games gold in Enduro X. She's used to winning, though. She came into the event as a 12-time world champ in trials riding.

* **Garrett Reynolds** won his sixth straight BMX Street gold medal. That puts him near the record set by his fellow BMX rider **Jamie Bestwick**, who has *eight* straight BMX Vert golds.

* Skateboard Park athlete **Alana Smith** didn't win gold, but a silver medal at age 12 made her the youngest athlete ever to finish top-three at an X Games.

Munich, Germany

* With yet another win in Skateboard Big Air, **Bob Burnquist** became the top X Games medalist of all-time. His gold gave him 25 medals in his career, one more than RallyCross driver **Dave Mirra**.

* **Brett Rheeder** won the first gold in the new Mountain Bike Slopestyle. His ride included back flips, tailwhips, and a "step-down," or drop, of more than 30 feet!

* **Chris Cole** won Street Skateboarding for the first time, beating longtime rival and former champion **Paul Rodriguez**.

* **Toomas Heikkinen** completed a full set of medals by earning gold in the action-packed RallyCross driving event. He had picked up a matching silver and bronze pair earlier in the summer. At 22, he's the youngest ever to medal in this grueling event.

Los Angeles, CA

* A new event, Gymkhana Grid, was added for the L.A. games. Combining rally driving, drifting, and a sort of obstacle course, Gymkhana Grid saw hot action and smoking tires. **Tanner Foust** won the gold-medal race.

* Moto X racing—bike-bumping, dirt-churning, high-flying action—also joined the sports list in L.A. with **Justin Brayton** coming out on top. **Vicki Golden** won the women's event.

* **Elliott Sloan** won his first X Games gold in Skateboard Big Air. He denied Bob Burnquist a chance at sweeping the X Games gold in 2013 in the event.

* Young and old: 16-year-old **Nyjah Huston** won gold in the Skateboard Street League, while 40-year-old Bucky Lasek completed a 2013 sweep of X Games gold in Skateboard Big Air.

* **Ronnie Renner** set a new record by winning his fifth straight Moto X Step Up event. He soared his bike 38.5 feet above the pole-vault-style jump.

This was the last X Games in L.A. To find out where they're moving, see page 141. For a complete list of winners at the 2013 Los Angeles X Games, please see page 143.

Winter X Games

Henrik Harlaut reached for the sky as he flipped and spun to silver in Slopestyle.

Aspen, Colorado

✳ Snowboarder **Elena Hight** stunned fans when she became the first rider, male or female, to land the difficult double backside alley-oop rodeo. But judges gave the SuperPipe gold medal to **Kelly Clark**, with Hight second. She'll always be the first to have landed that trick!

✳ **Henrik Harlaut** of Sweden also landed a unique trick—a nose butter triple cork 1620. The spectacular, twisting, flipping, spinning move in Slopestyle helped him win a silver medal.

✳ In the "no surprise" category, **Shaun White** won his sixth straight SuperPipe gold. The Flying Tomato has dominated

Sad News The 2013 action sports calendar started on a tragic note. Snowmobile stunt rider **Caleb Moore** was killed in a crash after his snowmobile landed on top of him in Aspen. The X Games soon canceled the snowmobile best trick and Moto X best trick events. Fellow athletes and fans were saddened by Moore's death.

the event since adding the snowboard to his awesome skateboarding skills.

✳ A pair of athletes each won a pair of golds—snowmobiler **Levi LaVallee** (Freestyle and Speed and Style) and snowboarder Louis-Felix Paradis (Real Snow and Street).

✳ **Tucker Hibbert** set a new mark for consecutive golds—he won his sixth straight Snowmobile SnoCross event. He also took home the championship in SnoCross, his seventh. He won his first when he was just 15!

For a complete list of X Games Aspen gold medal winners, please see page 142.

Tignes, France

✳ A Swiss snowboarder brought a couple of very well-known terms into the X Games in France. After a big snowstorm delayed the start of many events, **Iouri "I-Pod" Podladtchikov** became the first person ever to nail a Cab double cork 1440. At the SuperPipe event, he brought the crowd to its feet with his amazing trick, which he nicknamed "YOLO." Look for him to challenge the great Shaun White at the Olympics in Russia in 2014. **Louis Vito** ended up winning the event.

✳ Also at those Olympics, Ski SuperPipe will be competed for the first time. X Games fans in France got a preview as U.S. skier **Torin Yater-Wallace** won. He was closely trailed by hometown hero **Kevin Rolland** as well as the gold medalist from Aspen, **David Wise**.

✳ The best women's SuperPipe snowboarder ever continued her dominance. **Kelly Clark**, a former Olympic champion, won her record 62nd

event and third straight X Games gold. She had to battle that blizzard that hit near the start of these X Games.

✳ The French fans got a special treat at the Ski SuperPipe women's event. **Marie Martin-Routin**, who was coming back from retirement, won the gold. She credited the crowd with giving her the edge. "I heard you screaming and shouting so loud, it just gave me so much power," she said after getting her gold.

✳ Women's slopestyle saw a four-time champ crowned. Canada's **Kaya Turski** won for the fourth straight time.

✳ To compete in the men's Ski Slopestyle event, **McRae Williams** needed a little extra help. Due to the blizzard, his skis did not arrive on time. The airline bringing them lost his luggage! He had to scramble and have skis sent overnight. They arrived in time for him to qualify and he went on to win his first medal at an X Games.

Will "I-Pod" challenge White at the '14 Olympics?

Action Notes

McNamara earned a spot in Guinness Records by riding a 78-foot wave. But when he conquered a towering wall of water in Portugal on that January day, he became a surfing legend. McNamara became the first person to ride a wave estimated at more than 100 feet tall! The exact height has not been officially measured, but most experts think McNamara upped his record!

TOP ACTION SPORTS STARS: YOUR VOTES

ESPN put a stack of action sports stars into a months-long "playoff." Fans voted online for their favorites. Snowboarders faced off against skateboarders, while BMX riders sometimes "played" surfers. It was a wild-and-wacky contest, but in the end, two athletes came out on top.

MEN

Travis Rice, SNOWBOARD
2nd: **Torstein Horgmo**, SNOWBOARD

WOMEN

Grete Eliassen, SKIING
2nd: **Mimi Knoop**, SKATEBOARD

Monster Waves▲

▶ Heading into his ride off Portugal on January 29, 2013, surfer **Garrett McNamara** (above, on a smaller wave) was already a record-setter in big-wave surfing. In 2011,

DEW TOUR REPORT

The first of three Dew Tour events was held in Maryland in June 2013. The "Beach Championships," as this event was known, featured some big names and some up-and-coming stars. **Ryan Nyquist** (right) won the BMX Park, but **Dan Lacey** won the new Battle of the Beach event that combined various BMX styles. **Jamie Bestwick** won the BMX Vert, continuing a year of dominance for him. **Bucky Lasek** hoped to win the Skateboard Bowl in his home state, but **Pedro Barros** had such an awesome first run that Lasek couldn't knock him off the top spot. Lasek did win gold in the Vert, however. A special surprise was the Legends Bowl, in which some of skateboarding's all-time heroes took part. **Chris Miller** won, but every fan enjoyed seeing some of the guys who first took the sport worldwide.

▶ McNamara was taken into his wave while being towed by a jet-ski. But in December 2012, another surfer set a new record for biggest wave surfed after paddling in. Off the coast of northern California, **Shawn Dollar** conquered a 61-foot wave.

A Long Time in the Air

Dustin Martin and **Jonny Durand** had a record-setting airborne duel in the summer of 2012. In the skies over Texas, the two hang-gliders broke the record for longest flight. Martin went three miles further, however, and his 475-mile trip is now the world record. Each man flew south from near Lubbock for more than 11 hours. They landed near the Mexican border.

X Games New Home

For 11 years, the X Games have called Los Angeles home. X Games have been held in other places over the years, but the biggest events were always in sunny SoCal. In 2014, the X Games is moving to Austin, Texas. The wide-open spaces of the Lone Star State will give the X Games room for new tracks, new events, and new fans. Yee-ha!

2013 X Game Winners

BMX Big Air rider Morgan Wade soars above L.A., as the X Games say "so long" to California.

WINTER X GAMES
Aspen, Colorado

Snowmobile Freestyle
Levi LaVallee

Snowboard Street
Louis-Felix Paradis

Ski SuperPipe
(WOMEN)
Maddie Bowman

Snowboard Big Air
Torstein Horgmo

Ski SuperPipe
(MEN)
David Wise

Snowboard Slopestyle
(MEN)
Mark McMorris

Snowboard Slopestyle
(WOMEN)
Jamie Anderson

Snowmobile Speed & Style
Levi LaVallee

Ski Big Air
Henrik Harlaut

Snowboard SuperPipe
(WOMEN)
Kelly Clark

Ski Slopestyle
(MEN)
Nick Goepper

Ski Slopestyle
(WOMEN)
Tiril Sjastad Christiansen

Snowmobile SnoCross
Tucker Hibbert

Snowmobile Best Trick
Daniel Bodin

Snowboard SuperPipe
(MEN)
Shaun White

SUMMER X GAMES
Los Angeles, California

SLS Select Series
Ryan Decenzo

Skateboard Street
(WOMEN)
Leticia Bufoni

Skateboard Big Air
Elliot Sloan

Moto X Best Whip
Josh Hansen

Moto X Freestyle
Taka Hagashino

BMX Big Air
Morgan Wade

Moto X Step Up
Ronnie Renner

Moto X Speed & Style
Nate Adams

Skateboard Vert
Bucky Lasek

Street League Skateboard
Nyjah Huston

BMX Street
Chad Kerley

Gymkhana Grid
Tanner Foust

Moto X Racing
(MEN)
Justin Brayton

Moto X Racing
(WOMEN)
Vicky Golden

Enduro X
(MEN)
Taddy Blazusiak

Enduro X
(WOMEN)
Laia Sanz

RallyCross Lites
Joni Wiman

RallyCross SuperCar
Toomas Heikkinen

SOCCER

STAR OF TOMORROW
The young Brazilian forward known as Neymar scored a key goal to help his team beat Spain in the Confederations Cup. He'll play his pro soccer in Spain starting in 2013 but he'll have one eye on the World Cup, which Brazil will host in the summer of 2014.

World Cup Warm-Up

Brazil looks ready to rock in 2014 at the World Cup, which it will host. At the 2013 Confederations Cup, its national team put on a display of offensive brilliance and whomped Spain, 3–0. The Confederations Cup is held every four years, too, among the national-team champions from each of world soccer's geographic regions. In the final, young Brazilian superstar **Neymar** had a goal while **Fred** added two of his own. (As international soccer fans know, Brazilian players usually go by one-name nicknames.)

Spain, Brazil's opponent in the final, came into the event on a big roll, having won two European Championships and the 2010 World Cup. But Brazil came out strong and never let Spain get into its comfortable routine of passing and passing until its opponent broke down.

It was still an action-packed game, with both goalies making amazing saves. Perhaps the biggest save was by Brazilian defender **David Luiz**, who slid to the goal line to stop a Spanish shot that would have tied the game. After Spain lost a player to a red card, Brazil coasted home, to the delight of its fans.

Brazil will host the 2014 World Cup, so this Confederations Cup was a kind of warm-up for the organizers. Games were played in front of packed stadiums around the country. The Confederations final was held at the fabled Maracana Stadium in Rio de Janeiro. That will be the site of the World Cup final, too. As soccer fans count down the days until that big day, they can wonder: Was this Brazil-Spain game a preview of what they will see in 2014?

WHAT A YEAR!

Lionel Messi is clearly the best player in the world. He added to his amazing record in 2012 by scoring an all-time best 91 goals in all competitions. He beat the old single-year record of 86 set in 1972 by German hero **Gerd Müller**. Most of Messi's goals came during league and Cup games for his Spanish club team Barcelona. He also scored for his national team of Argentina. Here's the breakdown of Messi's magic:

GOALS	TEAM	EVENTS
59	Barcelona	La Liga
13	Barcelona	Champions League
12	Argentina	International games
7	Barcelona	Spanish cups

Champions League

Bayern (in red) won the German battle.

The annual UEFA Champions League came down to Spain vs. Germany—times two! After several months of intense games among Europe's top pro clubs, each semifinal matched a team from Spain's **La Liga** and a club from Germany's **Bundesliga**.

Barcelona made it to its semifinal in spectacular fashion. After losing the first game of a two-game series to Italy's AC Milan, "Barça" stormed back to win 4–0 and earn a spot in the semis. They were helped by the magical **Lionel Messi**, who scored a pair of goals in the second game.

When Barça faced off against German league champion **Bayern Munich**,

however, it was a different story. Bayern had played very well throughout the tournament, scoring often and playing tough D. Though many felt that Barcelona would win, Bayern Munich demolished the Spanish stars. In the two-game semifinal, they won by a total of 7–0. **Borussia Dortmund** won the other semifinal, but it was much closer. The German team won the first game against Real Madrid 4–1. In the second, however, Real won 2–0. By only one goal (4–3 total), Borussia made it an all-German championship game.

The two teams played a great game in London's Wembley Stadium. It was tied 1–1 until just two minutes left. That's when Bayern's **Arjen Robben**, who had missed several chances earlier, finally found the back of the net. His game-winner gave Bayern its first Champions League title since 2001.

GOLD CUP TRIUMPH!

The Gold Cup is held every two years among the national teams of CONCACAF, the region that includes North and Central America and the Caribbean. With a dominating offensive performance, the U.S. men's team won the 2013 Gold Cup. They scored a tournament-high 23 goals and went undefeated. In the final, **Brek Shea** knocked in the lone goal as the Americans beat Panama, 1–0.

Women's Soccer

The New Queen of Soccer

In 275 games for the U.S. women's soccer team, the great **Mia Hamm** scored 158 goals. With a goal against South Korea in her 207th international game, **Abby Wambach** (right) overcame Hamm and became the new scoring champ. The tall, powerful striker from upstate New York is now the world leader in goals scored by a woman. Wambach got world attention for her game-saving goal in the 2012 Olympics semifinals as well as helping the U.S. earn a runner-up spot in the 2011 Women's World Cup. After winning the 2012 FIFA Player of the Year award, she'll be a powerful presence in the new U.S. women's pro league (see box), but until then, she's happy as the world's best.

NEW WOMEN'S LEAGUE

Others have tried before and failed. But it's time to go back to the field for women's pro soccer in the U.S. The National Women's Soccer League (NWSL) started in July. With many of the top American players, including **Hope Solo** (Seattle), **Alex Morgan** (Portland), and **Abby Wambach** (Western New York) taking part, the league has high hopes of success. Top international players from Australia, Canada, Germany, and Mexico, among others, join U.S. players. Here's the list of teams for the league's first season:

Boston Breakers
Chicago Red Stars
FC Kansas City
Portland Thorns FC
Seattle Reign
Sky Blue FC
Washington Spirit
Western N.Y. Flash

MLS Report

The 2012 MLS season began with an international flair. The league added its third Canadian team, the Montreal Impact, and saw the first team from up north (the Vancouver Whitecaps) reach the playoffs. At midseason, those playoffs didn't look like they would include the defending champion L.A. Galaxy. The star-studded team won only three of its first 13 games. But after a break for the all-star game, the Galaxy sparkled, posting

2012 MLS AWARDS

MVP: **Chris Wondolowski,** SAN JOSE

ROOKIE OF THE YEAR: **Justin Berry,** CHICAGO

DEFENDER OF THE YEAR: **Matt Besler,** SPORTING KC

COMEBACK PLAYER OF THE YEAR: **Eddie Johnson,** SEATTLE

COACH OF THE YEAR: **Frank Yallop,** SAN JOSE

the league's best record in the second half.

Once the MLS playoffs began, there were a host of surprises. The team with the league's top record lost to a wild-card opponent, as Sporting Kansas City fell to the Houston Dynamo. The team that scored the most goals all season also lost when the San Jose Earthquakes fell to the Galaxy.

The MLS Cup came down to a repeat of the 2011 Cup–Galaxy vs. Dynamo.

Though Houston had an early 1–0 lead, the Galaxy had just too many weapons. U.S. national team sweeper **Omar Gonzalez** rose above a crowd of players in the 61st minute to head in the tying goal. Minutes later, the Galaxy forced a penalty kick, which **Landon Donovan** buried to take the lead. Near the end of the game, Irish national star and Galaxy scoring champ **Roy Keane** made a PK, too. After he banged it home, he performed his traditional double-somersault celebration to the delight of the hometown fans.

Helped by Donovan, English star **David Beckham** hoisted the MLS Cup for the second straight year . . . and for the last time. He announced soon after the game that he was leaving the Galaxy

Beckham bent his way to another title.

Wondo Ties Record

San Jose forward **Chris Wondolowski** grew up rooting for the Earthquakes. When they took him with the 41st pick of the 2005 draft, they probably didn't know they'd found a local hero. In 2012, "Wondo" tied an all-time league record with 27 goals. It was the third straight season he had lead MLS in goals. His MVP award after the season was the first given to an Earthquakes player and only the fifth ever to a U.S.-born star. He was also Player of the Month four times during the season. His play in MLS helped him earn more U.S. national team playing time. His five goals, including a hat trick against Belize, helped the U.S. win the 2013 Gold Cup.

(see box). Donovan tied a record with his fifth MLS title (two with San Jose and three with L.A.). His goal was also the 22nd he had scored in the MLS postseason, the most in league history. The Galaxy have now won four MLS Cups, tied with D.C. United for most all-time.

Bye-Bye, Beckham

The most famous soccer player in the world called it a career in early 2013. Free-kick superstar **David Beckham** had played for the L.A. Galaxy for five years after a world-class career with teams in England and Spain. He was one of only a few players to win league titles in four countries. He wrapped up his career with a few games with Paris St. Germain, with all of his salary going to children's charities.

MLS PLAYER COMES OUT

One of the biggest stories in the sports world in 2013 came from MLS. Shortly after NBA player **Jason Collins** came out as gay, former U.S. national soccer team midfielder **Robbie Rogers** did the same. When Rogers joined the Galaxy in May, Rogers became the first openly gay male player in a major American sport. (Collins was not signed with a team, so Rogers "beat" him to the field!) Collins and Rogers got tons of support from their teammates and fans. Rogers said, "It's been such a positive experience for me. I've learned from all of this that being gay is not that big of a deal to people."

Stat Stuff

MAJOR LEAGUE SOCCER
CHAMPIONS

2012	Los Angeles Galaxy
2011	Los Angeles Galaxy
2010	Colorado Rapids
2009	Real Salt Lake
2008	Columbus Crew
2007	Houston Dynamo
2006	Houston Dynamo
2005	Los Angeles Galaxy
2004	D.C. United
2003	San Jose Earthquakes
2002	Los Angeles Galaxy
2001	San Jose Earthquakes
2000	Kansas City Wizards
1999	D.C. United
1998	Chicago Fire
1997	D.C. United
1996	D.C. United

World Cup Scoring Leaders

MEN

GOALS	PLAYER, COUNTRY
15	Ronaldo, Brazil
14	Miroslav Klose, Germany
14	Gerd Müller, West Germany
13	Just Fontaine, France
12	Pelé, Brazil
11	Jürgen Klinsmann, Germany
11	Sandor Kocsis, Hungary

WOMEN

GOALS	PLAYER, COUNTRY
14	Birgit Prinz, Germany
14	Marta, Brazil
13	Abby Wambach, United States
12	Michelle Akers, United States

WOMEN'S WORLD CUP
ALL-TIME RESULTS

YEAR	CHAMPION	RUNNER-UP
2011	**Japan**	United States
2007	**Germany**	Brazil
2003	**Germany**	Sweden
1999	**United States**	China
1995	**Norway**	Germany
1991	**United States**	Norway

UEFA CHAMPIONS LEAGUE

The Champions League pits the best against the best. The top club teams from the members of UEFA (Union of European Football Associations) face off in a months-long tournament. They squeeze the games in among their regular league games, so the winners need to be talented and extremely fit. Read about the 2013 winner on page 146. Here are other recent Champions League champions!

2013 Bayern Munich/GERMANY

2012 Chelsea FC/ENGLAND

2011 FC Barcelona/SPAIN

2010 Inter (Milan)/ITALY

2009 FC Barcelona/SPAIN

2008 Manchester United/ENGLAND

2007 AC Milan/ITALY

2006 FC Barcelona/SPAIN

2005 Liverpool FC/ENGLAND

2004 FC Porto/PORTUGAL

2003 AC Milan/ITALY

2002 Real Madrid/SPAIN

2001 Bayern Munich/GERMANY

2000 Real Madrid/SPAIN

GOLF

PARK POWER!
Inbee Park was the biggest success story in golf in 2013. The Korean native became the first female golfer to win the first three major championships of the year since 1950.

Tee-off Time

Though the 2012 golf season saw a bit of a comeback by **Tiger Woods**, the big star of that year was another young star. **Rory McIlroy** won six events on the PGA Tour, plus two more in Europe. He led the PGA in scoring average, and was No. 2 in the all-around. He finished the year ranked No. 1 in the world, too. Though the first part of 2013 was not as strong for the golfer from Northern Ireland, he has placed himself firmly among the stars to watch in the future.

Woods, of course, has not gone away. He continued to be the man to beat on the PGA Tour, earning all the headlines. He won five tournaments in the early part of 2013, including his second Players Championship. Whenever he was in a tournament, his performance was the main story, with the winners often getting second billing. Through the 2013 British Open, he had not won a major in more than three years, but he remains golf's biggest name.

Golf's biggest prizewinner, however, was **Brendt Snedeker**. Overcoming some long odds, the young golfer from Tennessee earned $10 million for winning the 2012 FedEx Cup. The season-ending series matches the best golfers from the season. Woods and McIlroy were joined by superstars like **Phil Mickelson** and **Lee Westwood** in the event. However, Snedeker ended up on top and took home the big check.

In 2013, the list of Majors winners added two new names. **Adam Scott** became the first player from Australia to win the Masters. Scott beat **Angel Cabrera** in a playoff to win the green jacket. At the U.S. Open, **Justin Rose** ended another long streak. The native of England was the first from his country to win the Open since 1970. A disappointed Phil Mickelson finished second for the sixth time after leading during the final round.

At the British Open, however, Mickelson turned that disappointment to joy. In one of the biggest final-round comebacks ever, he came from five strokes back to win his first British Open. His 66 was the best he had ever done in the final round of a major event.

As good as McIlroy and Woods were and as happy as fans were for "Lefty" Mickelson, perhaps the biggest story in golf was on the women's side. Korean golfer **Inbee Park** became the first LPGA player since 1950 to win the season's first three majors. Read more about her amazing season on page 157.

2013 MEN'S MAJORS

THE MASTERS
Adam Scott

THE U.S. OPEN
Justin Rose

THE BRITISH OPEN
Phil Mickelson

THE PGA CHAMPIONSHIP
Jason Dufner

Ryder Collapse

The Ryder Cup is played every two years between teams of golfers from the U.S. and Europe. At the 2012 event, not even having **Tiger Woods** on its side was enough for the U.S. squad. In a stunning upset, the Europeans came from behind to capture the Cup on the final day, 14.5 to 13.5. (Each of the three days of the event includes several matches between singles or pairs of players. Each match is worth one point.)

On the final Sunday, the U.S. team led by four points. They needed to win only five of the 12 singles matches to clinch the Cup. Instead, they earned only 3.5 points. Six of the 12 matches on Sunday went to the final hole . . . and U.S. golfers lost or tied all of them. German golfer **Martin Kaymer** made a birdie putt to beat **Steve Stricker** to give Europe the win.

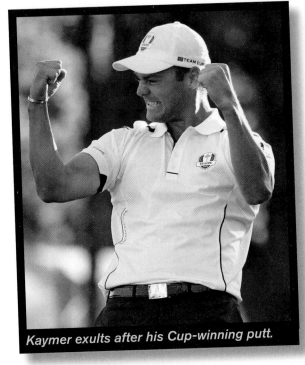

Kaymer exults after his Cup-winning putt.

The comeback tied the biggest ever in the Ryder Cup, which was first played back in in 1927. The U.S. team pulled off a similar comeback in 1999.

The 2012 European squad was inspired by Spanish golfer **Seve Ballesteros**, a legendary champion and former Ryder Cup captain who had died a year earlier. England's **Ian Poulter** was one of the biggest stars, going 4-0 in his matches.

2012 U.S. RYDER CUP TEAM

Keegan Bradley	Phil Mickelson
Jason Dufner	Webb Simpson
Jim Furyk	Brandt Snedeker
Dustin Johnson	Steve Stricker
Zach Johnson	Bubba Watson
Matt Kuchar	Tiger Woods

Park Power!

Heading into 2013, the LPGA Tour certainly knew who **Inbee Park** was. In 2008, she was only 19 when she won the U.S. Women's Open, the youngest ever to earn that honor. In 2012, she won a pair of events and finished second in six others. In 2013, however, she vaulted to new heights. Among her first five victories were the Kraft Nabisco Championship and the LPGA Championship, two of the LPGA's five Majors. But she was just getting started. In July she won her second career U.S. Open, giving her the first three majors of the year. No LPGA golfer had done that since the great **Babe Didrikson Zaharias** way back in 1950! Park was the first golfer to win three in one season since **Pat Bradley** in 1986, but Bradley did not go back-to-back-to-back!

"Trying to put my name next to [Zaharias] means just so much," Park said. "I would think I would never get there; it's somewhere that I've never dreamed of. But all of a sudden, I'm there."

Before Park began her record run, an American golfer did make some news. In March 2013 **Stacy Lewis** won the LPGA Founders Cup. The victory earned her enough points to jump to No. 1 in the world. That knocked **Yani Tseng** from the top spot that she had held for more than two years. Lewis became only the seventh woman at the top of the world rankings. In August, Lewis won the Women's British Open to snap Park's majors streak.

SOLHEIM CUP

The Solheim Cup pits teams of top female U.S. golfers against European golfers. The 2013 event was held in Colorado, and Europe won for the first time in America. The first day, they went ahead 5–3 (each match is worth a point) and then dominated Saturday's four-ball play, winning every point. Europe kept it up on Sunday, earning seven more points. Europe's 18–10 win was the biggest in Solheim Cup history. Sweden's **Caroline Hedwall** was the star for Europe, winning all five of her matches.

Chip Shots

Courage on the Greens

PGA golfer **Charlie Beljan** thrilled golf fans when he won his first PGA Tour event, the 2012 Children's Miracle Network Hospitals Classic in Florida. He won despite having a severe panic attack during Friday's round. He had to spend that night in the hospital, but crawled from his bed to carry on to victory on Sunday.

> **"I was just thinking about my health, one shot at a time, one hole at a time. And shoot, it worked out pretty well."**
>
> — GOLFER CHARLIE BELJAN
> AFTER BATTLING PANIC ATTACKS ON THE WAY TO WINNING

Just Missed!

At the 2013 Phoenix Open, **Phil Mickelson** came within a whisker of scoring the magical 59. Only five golfers have had a score that low in a PGA event. Mickelson barely missed a final putt and ended up with a 60.

Wrong Ball?

While playing in the Phoenix Open, **Padraig Harrington** got his gear mixed up. Thanks to a sponsor, he paused at one hole to punt some footballs into the crowd! Harrington finished tied for ninth, however, 12 shots behind the amazing Mickelson.

◀◀◀Two for the Teens

In April, **Guan Tianlang** became the youngest player ever to play in the Masters. He was just 14! He earned his spot by winning

◀◀◀Was He Aiming for the Pool?

The world knows **Michael Phelps** as the most decorated Olympian of all time. But the swimmer retired and took up golf in 2012. Playing at an event in Scotland, he made an amazing 159-foot putt! It took 17 seconds to run all the way across the green before "diving" into the hole!

How Big Is the Bag?

In late 2012, a golf pro named **Michael Furrh** hit a drive 146 yards. Not very good, right? But consider that he was using the world's longest golf club! Furrh's driver measured 14 feet, 2.5 inches, setting a new world record.

a big amateur event in China. In the 2013 Masters, he finished 58th, but was the lowest-scoring amateur player there, which earned him a special award. Then, in July, **Jordan Smith** was just 19 when he won the John Deere Classic. He was the youngest to win a PGA Tour event in 82 years!

OTHER WINNERS

The PGA Tour is not the only place for top golfers. Here are some quick looks at other 2012 stars.

Champions Tour

Founded in 1980, this is for golfers 50 and over. In 2012, Germany's **Bernhard Langer** finished first on the money list with more than $2 million in earnings. He joined many other former PGA Tour stars keeping their pro golf game going on the Champions Tour.

Web.com Tour

Though it has had several names over the years, this series of tournaments is sort of like the minor leagues for the PGA Tour. Golfers hope to earn enough points to move up to the big tour. In 2012, **Casey Wittenberg** ended up on top of this tour. He and 24 other golfers got to move up to the top!

The Majors

In golf, some tournaments are known as the majors. They're the four most important events of the year on either the men's or the women's pro tours. **Tiger Woods** has the most career wins in majors among current golfers. **Annika Sörenstam** retired in 2010 with the most among recent **LPGA** players.

MEN'S

	MASTERS	U.S. OPEN	BRITISH OPEN	PGA CHAMP.	TOTAL
Jack **NICKLAUS**	6	4	3	5	18
Tiger **WOODS**	4	3	3	4	14
Walter **HAGEN**	0	2	4	5	11
Ben **HOGAN**	2	4	1	2	9
Gary **PLAYER**	3	1	3	2	9
Tom **WATSON**	2	1	5	0	8
Arnold **PALMER**	4	1	2	0	7
Gene **SARAZEN**	1	2	1	3	7
Sam **SNEAD**	3	0	1	3	7
Harry **VARDON**	0	1	6	0	7

RYDER CUP

The past ten winners of the Ryder Cup

2012: EUROPE
2010: EUROPE
2008: UNITED STATES

2006: EUROPE
2004: EUROPE
2002: EUROPE
1999: UNITED STATES

1997: EUROPE
1995: EUROPE
1993: UNITED STATES

WOMEN'S

	LPGA	USO	BO	NAB	MAUR	TH	WES	TOTAL
Patty **BERG**	0	1	x	x	x	7	7	15
Mickey **WRIGHT**	4	4	x	x	x	2	3	13
Louise **SUGGS**	1	2	x	x	x	4	4	11
Annika **SÖRENSTAM**	3	3	1	3	x	x	x	10
Babe **ZAHARIAS**	x	3	x	x	x	3	4	10
Betsy **RAWLS**	2	4	x	x	x	x	2	8
Juli **INKSTER**	2	2	x	2	1	x	x	7
Karrie **WEBB**	1	2	1	2	1	x	x	7

KEY: LPGA = LPGA Championship, USO = U.S. Open, BO = British Open, NAB = Nabisco Championship, MAUR = du Maurier (1979–2000), TH = Titleholders (1937–1972), WES = Western Open (1937–1967)

PGA TOUR CAREER EARNINGS*

1. Tiger Woods — $107,109,819
2. Phil Mickelson — $72,505,508
3. Vijay Singh — $67,571,945
4. Jim Furyk — $53,874,638
5. Ernie Els — $45,715,500
6. Davis Love III — $42,494,966
7. David Toms — $39,124,289
8. Steve Stricker — $37,386,307
9. Justin Leonard — $32,519,857
10. Sergio Garcia — $32,040,396

LPGA TOUR CAREER EARNINGS*

1. Annika Sörenstam — $22,573,192
2. Karrie Webb — $17,967,981
3. Cristie Kerr — $14,867,341
4. Lorena Ochoa — $14,863,331
5. Juli Inkster — $13,525,568

* Through July 2013

KARRIE WEBB

The Australian-born Webb is the only golfer on the list above who still is active on a full slate of tournaments. She burst onto the LPGA scene at the age of 21 and won all of her majors in her first decade on the tour. She was No. 2 in the world for most of a decade and is still ranked No. 8 in the world, nearly 20 years after starting out. Few golfers have had careers as long or as steady as Webb. She's already in the LPGA Hall of Fame, but she's still out there every weekend trying to add to her amazing record.

TENNIS

Andy Murray became the first person from Great Britain to win the Wimbledon Championships since 1936. He celebrated with his home country fans after beating Novak Djokovic.

Men's Tennis

For the first time in a long time, the big name in men's tennis was not **Federer**, **Nadal**, or **Djokovic**. With his first victory at Wimbledon—and the first by a British player in 77 years—**Andy Murray** became the toast of the tennis world.

Murray beat Novak Djokovic in straight sets, thrilling the huge crowd at the stadium near London. Murray had finished as the 2012 runner-up and had come close other times, so this was a huge relief. Wimbledon remains one of the premier events in the sports world, so British fans were getting desperate to have one of their own hoist the trophy.

To reach the historic day, Murray and Djokovic avoided a string of upsets that knocked out other top players (see page 163). In the final, Murray used a powerful, accurate serve to control the match. The last game of the third set, however, drained him. "At the end, mentally, that last game will be the toughest game I'll play in my entire career, ever," Murray said.

With the championship, he became the first Briton since **Fred Perry** in 1936 to win it all. It also capped off a year in which

Nadal continued his domination on clay.

Murray won the 2012 Olympic gold medal, also in London, and then his first U.S. Open.

Meanwhile, Rafael Nadal, the Spanish star, made his own news. With his eighth French Open title, he set a new record for most titles in a Grand Slam event. Roger Federer and **Pete Sampras** each won seven Wimbledons, and **Bill Tilden** won seven U.S. Opens. Nadal later won the U.S. Open, moving him into third place for career Grand Slams. He was the only player with two Grand Slams in 2013, and he was perfect on hardcourts. Murray is rising, but Nadal and Djokovic won't fall easily.

2013 MEN'S GRAND SLAMS

AUSTRALIAN OPEN	**Novak Djokovic**
FRENCH OPEN	**Rafael Nadal**
WIMBLEDON	**Andy Murray**
U.S. OPEN	**Rafael Nadal**

Women's Tennis

Serena Williams was the big story in women's tennis—again. Whether losing at the Australian Open, winning the French, being upset at Wimbledon, or dominating at the U.S. Open, she was the player to watch—and to beat—all year long.

Already one of the greatest players ever, Williams added to her record with her 16th Grand Slam win at the French Open in June. Her overpowering serve and athletic abilities made her an unstoppable force at that tournament, and she continued to dominate the women's tour for weeks afterward. Before falling in a big shocker at Wimbledon,

A win at the French Open started Serena's great year.

2013 WOMEN'S GRAND SLAMS

AUSTRALIAN OPEN	**Victoria Azarenka**
FRENCH OPEN	**Serena Williams**
WIMBLEDON	**Marion Bartoli**
U.S. OPEN	**Serena Williams**

she had won 34 straight matches.

Williams was not the only top player to struggle at Wimbledon. Just as in the men's draw, the top women players fell left and right. No. 2 **Victoria Azarenka** and No. 9 **Caroline Wozniacki** left with injuries. No. 3 **Maria Sharapova** and No. 5 **Sara Errani** lost early. No. 10 **Maria Kirilenko** lost to British favorite **Laura Robson**. Williams, at No. 1, lost in the quarterfinals to 23rd-seeded German **Sabine Lisicki**. When the dust had cleared, the finals were between Lisicki and No. 15 **Marion Bartoli** of France, the highest seeding combo ever in the Open era (since 1968). Bartoli won in two sets. "You cannot describe my feelings," a stunned Bartoli said. "You cannot put any words what I'm feeling at this moment."

However, the upset at Wimbledon was forgotten as she stormed through the U.S. Open to win her 17th Grand Slam championship.

TENNIS NOTES

Two for the Record ▶

Doubles tennis doesn't get the headlines that singles gets. Most pros specialize in playing singles or doubles. Doubles teams need to think together, act quickly, and have perfect strategy, along with great tennis skills. Mike (left) and Bob Bryan might have a little advantage there: They're twin brothers! At the 2013 Australian Open, the Bryans won their 13th

Grand Slam doubles championship, the most ever by one team. The record has lasted since the late 1960s. With wins in the French Open and at Wimbledon, they became the first doubles team since 1968 to hold all four Grand Slam titles at once.

Blow Up at Wimbledon 2013

Coming into Wimbledon, Rafael Nadal had recently won the French Open . . . again. He was ranked No. 2 in the world. Belgium's Steve Darcis was ranked No. 135 when he upset Nadal at Wimbledon. It was one of the biggest upsets ever at the tournament and the first time that Nadal had ever lost in a Grand Slam opening match. It was the start of a run of upsets that left only the top two seeds in the quarterfinals.

◀ Rising Star

At the Australian Open, Serena Williams was upset by another American, 19-year-old Sloane Stephens. Is she the next American tennis star? Sloane grew up in Florida and started playing tennis when she was nine. Sloane's mother was a college swimming star and her late father played in the NFL. Sloane's big win in Australia helped her reach the top 20 worldwide for the first time.

Grand Slams

ALL-TIME GRAND SLAM CHAMPIONSHIPS (MEN)

	AUS. OPEN	FRENCH OPEN	WIMBLEDON	U.S. OPEN	TOTAL
Roger **FEDERER**	4	1	7	5	17
Pete **SAMPRAS**	2	0	7	5	14
Rafael **NADAL**	1	8	2	2	13
Roy **EMERSON**	6	2	2	2	12
Björn **BORG**	0	6	5	0	11
Rod **LAVER**	3	2	4	2	11
Bill **TILDEN**	0	0	3	7	10
Jimmy **CONNORS**	1	0	2	5	8
Ivan **LENDL**	2	3	0	3	8
Fred **PERRY**	1	1	3	3	8
Ken **ROSEWALL**	4	2	0	2	8
Andre **AGASSI**	4	1	1	2	8

IVAN LENDL
The success of Scotsman Andy Murray brought Lendl back into the spotlight. The former No. 1 tennis star is Murray's coach. Lendl can draw on a great career record to help his younger student. A native of Czechoslovakia, Lendl reached No. 1 for the first time in 1983. He won the 1984 French Open, the first of eight Grand Slams he would win, including three straight U.S. Opens. He also reached the finals of Grand Slam events a record-tying 19 times.

ALL-TIME GRAND SLAM CHAMPIONSHIPS (WOMEN)

	AUS.	FRENCH	WIMBLEDON	U.S.	TOTAL
Margaret Smith **COURT**	11	5	3	5	24
Steffi **GRAF**	4	6	7	5	22
Helen Wills **MOODY**	0	4	8	7	19
Chris **EVERT**	2	7	3	6	18
Martina **NAVRATILOVA**	3	2	9	4	18
Serena **WILLIAMS**	5	2	5	5	17
Billie Jean **KING**	1	1	6	4	12
Maureen **CONNOLLY**	1	2	3	3	9
Monica **SELES**	4	3	0	2	9
Suzanne **LENGLEN**	0	2*	6	0	8
Molla Bjurstedt **MALLORY**	0	0	0	8	8

*Also won 4 French titles before 1925; in those years, the tournament was open only to French nationals.

CAREER GRAND SLAMS

(Year represents fourth win of four Grand Slam events. Players with an * also won an Olympic gold medal.)

Maria SHARAPOVA (2012)

Serena WILLIAMS* (2003)

Steffi GRAF* (1988)

Martina NAVRATILOVA (1983)

Chris EVERT (1982)

Billie Jean KING (1972)

Margaret SMITH COURT (1963)

Shirley Fry IRVIN (1957)

Maureen CONNOLLY (1953)

Doris HART (1954)

OTHER SPORTS

With American skiing superstar Lindsey Vonn out for most of the year, Slovenia's Tina Maze (pictured) took advantage. Maze was the overall World Cup skiing champion for the first time, while also winning three individual events. Check out more of her feats, and get a preview of the 2014 Winter Olympics stars on page 168.

Winter Sports

SKIING

Just when everyone thought American superstar **Lindsey Vonn** was the best skier on the planet, along came Slovenia's **Tina Maze**. While Vonn dealt with a virus and then a knee injury that kept her out for several months, Maze put together one of the best World Cup seasons ever. She won the overall championship with a record-setting 2,414 points, more than twice as many as runner-up **Maria Hoefl-Riesch**. Maze also won three individual events: giant slalom, Super-G, and combined.

After winning four World Cup overall titles, Vonn was disappointed by her 2013 season. However, she was successful enough in her downhill runs before her accident that she captured yet another world title in that high-speed discipline. Vonn did get a bit lucky, however. The final event, at which Maze needed only one point to overcome Vonn's downhill lead, was cancelled by bad weather. Vonn's 17th World Cup championship set a new all-time record as well.

U.S. skier **Julia Mancuso** finished fourth overall in the World Cup standings, just ahead of fellow American and teenage sensation **Mikaela Shiffrin**. Shiffrin's overall championship in the slalom was a huge surprise, and she had to beat Maze to earn it. At 18, Shiffrin was the first American

American slalom star Ted Ligety was the first triple World Champion in 45 years!

woman in 29 years to win the difficult slalom event and the youngest overall in 39 years!

All of this World Cup action by a host of top skiers means that the women's skiing events at the 2014 Winter Olympics should be fantastic.

Ted Ligety is an American male skier with great hopes for Sochi, Russia, site of those Winter Games. At the 2013 World Championships in February, Ligety won three events—giant slalom, Super-G, and super-combined. Ligety was the first man to win three since the great French champion **Jean-Claude Killy** way back in 1968. Though Ligety was not exactly an underdog, he had never won any World Championship events before his historic week of Ws. On the World Cup circuit, he also won the season-long giant slalom event and finished third in the overall.

Patrick Chan

FIGURE SKATING

Home cooking must have tasted pretty good to **Patrick Chan** (left). At the 2013 World Figure Skating Championships in Ontario, Canada, Chan was the home-country favorite. He skated beautifully in the first round and set a world record for points. Even though he stumbled and fell in the free skate, he held on to win his third straight world championship.

The women's champion was another familiar face, **Yu-Na Kim** of South Korea, the 2010 Olympic gold medalist. After her triumph in Vancouver, she took almost two years off. She was certainly not rusty for the 2013 Worlds, however. She skated flawlessly and beat Italy's **Carolina Kostner** by more than 20 points. American skaters got good news, too. Thanks to **Ashley Wagner** (fifth) and **Gracie Gold** (sixth), the U.S. will be able to send three skaters to the 2014 Winter Olympics.

The pairs competition saw more world records fall. The amazing Russian team of **Tatiana Volosozhar** and **Maxim Trankov** scored record points in the free skate and the total. Next year at the Winter Games, *they'll* have the home-ice advantage.

In the ice dance, even skating in their home province of Ontario was not enough to help **Tessa Virtue** and **Scott Moir**. The defending world champs were overcome by their longtime rivals from the United States, **Meryl Davis** and **Charlie White**. The two pairs have dominated recent world championships and figure to battle to the end for gold in Russia.

IDITAROD

The coldest race in the world ended with the oldest champ ever in the lead. The Iditarod sled-dog race challenges man and beast across icy Alaska. It was created in honor of a long-ago sled-dog relay that brought life-saving medicine to an isolated town. **Mitch Seavey** and his 10 dogs won the 2013 race in nine days, seven hours, and 39 minutes. At 53, Seavey was the oldest winner yet; he also won the race in 2004 . . . and his son won in 2012!

Horseracing

The annual Triple Crown races are the highlight of every year's horse racing calendar. Though some people follow the sport year-round, the Triple Crown races catch the attention of the entire sports world. The 2013 races were no exception, providing drama and heartbreak as usual.

As the field in the 139th Kentucky Derby charged for the finish line, thousands of fans were very worried. They had made **Orb** the favorite in the

Orb (right) splashed through the Kentucky mud.

race, but at the final turn, the horse was far behind. Jockey **Joel Rosario** was right where he wanted to be, however. As the leaders bunched together on the rail, he steered Orb outside. The horse pounded past the field and won in a thrilling finish. **Rosie Napravnik** also made history at this year's Derby. Her fifth-place finish on **Mylute** was the highest ever by a woman jockey in the Derby. (She also rode in the other Triple Crown races in 2013, the first time a woman has done that, too!)

In the Preakness, most people thought Orb would sail to victory again. But jockey **Gary Stevens** showed why he is one of the best of all time. His ride on **Oxbow** to win the Preakness was a thing of beauty, charging to the lead early and staying there all the way to the finish line. He and Oxbow beat the heavy favorite, who finished fourth. The win gave Stevens nine victories in Triple Crown races.

The third leg of the Triple Crown is the longest and hardest race. The Belmont Stakes calls for horses to race 1.5 miles at the end of a long season of racing. The difficult race is a big reason there has not been a Triple Crown winner (that is, all three races in one year) since 1978. At the 2013 Belmont, a horse that had finished 12th in the Kentucky Derby ended up the winner. **Palace Malice**, with jockey **Mike Smith**, was a 13-1 underdog, but charged past Oxbow in the home stretch to win easily.

Track & Field

At the United States Track and Field Championships in June in Iowa, several American records fell and the top U.S. athletes showed off their skills running, jumping, and throwing.

* **Tyson Gay** ran the fastest 100- and 200-meter times of the year while capturing the sprint double.

* **Ashton Eaton** *(above)*, the Olympic gold medalist in the decathlon, continued his domination, winning the American title. **Sharon Day** was the heptathlon champion.

* The women's 200-meter run saw an upset, as gold medalist **Allyson Felix** lost to **Kimberly Duncan** by 0.05 seconds.

* **Matthew Centrowitz** held off a tight pack of finishers in the men's 1,500-meter run. He was first, but five other runners finished within a second of him. In the women's race, **Trenier Moser** nipped **Mary Cain** at the wire to win by less than a second.

* In the throwing events, fans saw two new American records. **Amanda Bingson** sent the hammer flying 245, five inches, while **Michelle Carter** put the shot 66 feet, 5 inches. Both were new U.S. marks, and Carter earned her fourth U.S. outdoor championship.

Lacrosse

North Carolina won its first title with an overtime upset.

NCAA

Duke University found itself in a big hole at the 2013 NCAA men's lacrosse championship. In the second quarter, Duke trailed Syracuse 5–0. Part of the reason was that Duke missed its first 11 shots on goal.

But Duke slowly rallied back, led by faceoff man **Brendan Fowler**. In lacrosse, winning faceoffs after goals or fouls is important. By winning the faceoff, you control the ball and have the best chance to score. At one stretch, Fowler won 13 faceoffs in a row. With that edge, they tied the game at 7–7 and then just kept rolling. The final score was 16–10, giving Duke its second national title.

The women's NCAA title game was even more exciting. Maryland entered the contest against North Carolina as the overwhelming favorite. They had not lost in 2013 and had won 10 previous national titles. They had also beaten North Carolina twice already! But the Tar Heels took the game to overtime. In the third extra period, **Sammy Jo Tracy** scored for North Carolina and the upset was complete. It was the Tar Heels' first-ever title in women's lacrosse.

National Lacrosse League

It was a different year, but the same result in the pro indoor lacrosse championship. The Rochester Knighthawks won their second straight NLL title, holding on for dear life to defeat the Washington Stealth. At a sold-out arena in British Columbia, the two teams were neck-and-neck throughout the game. Rochester clung to a one-goal lead for the last several minutes, as the Stealth tried for the tying goal. But Knighthawks goalie **Matt Vinc** did his best impression of a brick wall and Rochester held on for the victory.

Cycling

The 2013 Tour de France was the 100th running of the world's most famous cycling race. In the first 98 of them, no riders from Great Britain had ever won. **Bradley Wiggins** broke that streak in 2012, and **Chris Froome** kept it going in 2013. The powerful Froome grabbed the lead after the eighth stage of the 21-stage, 2,115-mile race . . . and he never let it go. Through the mountains and during days of sprints he held on to the famous yellow jersey given to the race leader. He also avoided several big, multi-rider crashes that hit the race early on. Froome finished more than five minutes ahead of second-place finisher **Nairo Quintana** of Colombia, the biggest margin of victory since 1997. With the ongoing fallout from **Lance Armstrong** (see box) and other cyclists' drug use, Froome and his open, positive attitude seem like a clean and healthy new start for a new century of the Tour de France.

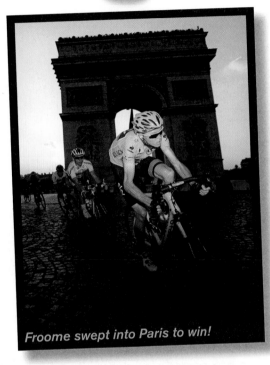

Froome swept into Paris to win!

ARMSTRONG CONFESSES

On January 13, 2013, on *Oprah's Next Chapter*, cycling star **Lance Armstrong** confessed to using performance-enhancing drugs (PEDs) many times during his career. The news was shocking, mostly because Armstrong had spent years denying that he had used drugs. He was stripped of his records. Several other cyclists had been caught using PEDs, but Armstrong never

had. However, American and international investigators had pretty much proven that he did. They officially charged him in the fall of 2012. When he refused to defend the charges, he finally decided to come clean.

Armstrong had won a record seven Tour de France races and become an international sports superstar. He had also battled back from cancer and started Livestrong, a group that raises money to fight the disease. His good works made his longtime lies that much bigger news and disappointed millions.

Swimming

Missy made a big splash at the Worlds.

won the 200-meter backstroke, 4x200 freestyle relay, 200-meter freestyle, 100-meter backstroke, and 4x100-meter freestyle. That last medal was the first gold for the U.S. women in the event since 2003. Then, in the 4x100-meter medley relay, Franklin got her record sixth. That also gave her nine career golds, setting another record.

Franklin was not the only women's star. **Katie Ledecky**, who was only 16 at this event, won four gold medals. She became only the second swimmer ever to win the 400-, 800-, and 1500-meter events at one World Championships. And she set new world records in the 800 and 1500!

Ruta Meilutyte gave Lithuania its first World Championship gold medal by winning the 100-meter breaststroke. She also set a world record in the semifinal.

On the men's side, **Ryan Lochte** was the U.S. star. He won the 200-meter individual medley, the 200-meter backstroke, and helped win the 4x200 freestyle relay. The medals gave him an amazing career total of 23 at the Worlds. China's **Yang Sun** matched Ledecky's feat by winning all three freestyle distance races.

With the great **Michael Phelps** now retired, South Africa's **Chad Le Clos** took over as world champ in the butterfly events, winning the 100- and 200-meter races.

The success of Franklin, Lochte, and their teammates placed the U.S. first in overall medals. They brought home 29, including 13 gold. China was second with nine medals (five gold), while France also had nine medals, but only four gold.

Missy Franklin was the female swimming star of the 2012 London Olympics with four gold medals. After those Games, she decided to head to the University of California. After a fun freshman year, she showed that she was still among the world's best. At the 2013 World Swimming and Diving Championships, Franklin became the first woman ever to capture six gold medals at the event. She

Cricket

You might not have seen these cricket highlights on ESPN, but more than a billion people around the world did. Though the sport has not caught on in the U.S., it's HUGE worldwide. Two events caught the attention of the cricket world in the past year:

✳ A version of cricket called Twenty20 (T20) has become very popular. Unlike international matches, which can last five days (really!), T20 games are much quicker. At the 2012 World T20 event, a surprise winner emerged from more than two weeks of hotly-contested matches. The West Indies team, led by batters **Marlon Samuels** and **Darren Sammy**, defeated Sri Lanka in the championship match. It was the first world title for the team, which includes players from several Caribbean nations, since 1979.

✳ A member of that West Indies team made headlines of his own in April 2013. Playing for his club team in the Indian Premier League, one of the top pro circuits, **Chris Gayle** scored a century in only 30 bowls! Okay, so that might need a translation. In cricket, the bowler is like the pitcher; he throws the ball toward the batsman, who whacks the ball to the field. Different hits earn different points. The best is for six points, like a home run. Gayle had 11 sixes on his way to his first 100 points (called a century) on only 30 pitches, the fastest anyone has ever done that. He ended his "innings" (time at bat) with another record, 175 points, before being put out. This was huge news everywhere but here!

Gayle made cricket history twice in '12–13.

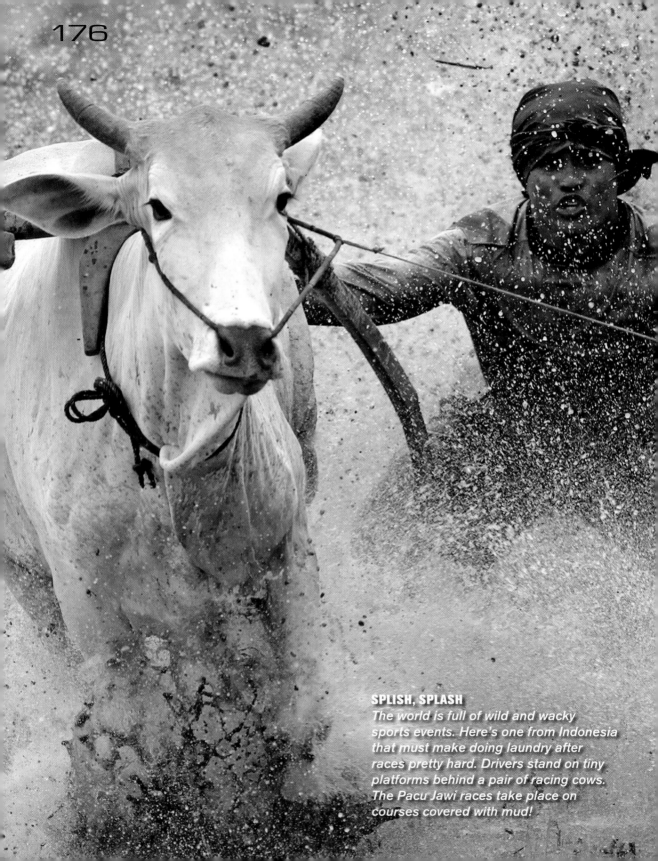

SPLISH, SPLASH

The world is full of wild and wacky sports events. Here's one from Indonesia that must make doing laundry after races pretty hard. Drivers stand on tiny platforms behind a pair of racing cows. The Pacu Jawi races take place on courses covered with mud!

AMAZING SPORTS

Chess King!

Chess does not get a lot of coverage in the sports world, but it's a huge international competition with winners and losers and rankings. So we think this news fits into our reporting on Amazing Sports. In 2013, Norwegian player **Magnus Carlsen** became the highest-rated player of all time! His total of 2,861 career points beat out the old record set by **Garry Kasparov**. Magnus, who is only 22, is the three-time player of the year and is the man to beat in any competition he enters.

Flying Flowers

Look, up in the sky! It's a bird! It's a plane! It's . . . a flower? A new world record was set in Russia when 101 skydivers, all female, combined to form a gigantic flying flower. After plummeting out of a plane, they guided their bodies together. Linking up by arms and feet, they formed a huge flower shape for several moments. Then they all let go, pulled their ripcords, and floated to earth.

Quidditch World Cup VI

You probably didn't even know there was a Quidditch World Cup, but 2013 was the sixth annual edition! The sport was inspired, of course, by the Harry Potter books. College students have been running (but not flying) around with brooms trying to catch a very mobile Snitch for more than a decade. Students at Middlebury College in Vermont get the credit for starting the college competitions. Middlebury won the first five World Cups, but in 2013, a new champ emerged. The University of Texas outscored UCLA in the final, 190–80, clinching their win by snagging the Snitch. Got some brooms at home? Why not try it out and we'll see you in the World Cup in a few years.

Broomsticks and Quaffles mean intense Quidditch action!

Trampoline dodgeball is played at special gyms caled SkyZones that have walls and floors made of trampolines. Players leap and bounce around while they catch and throw rubber balls at each other. There was even a world championship in Los Angeles in 2012. The best way to try is to find a trampoline gym near you and start bouncing!

Rollerman▲

You've seen in-line roller skates, right? A few wheels on the bottom of skate-like shoes. Well, a French designer named Jean-Yves "Rollerman" Blondeau thought that was just not enough. A few years ago, he developed an entire suit of roller wheels. He's up to 31 different wheels on his chest, arms, knees, hands, and legs. Using this wheel-covered suit (and yes, a helmet!), he can whiz downhill up to 70 mph! The space-age suit has appeared in a 2013 movie with Jackie Chan and in commercials around the world. He also slid down the Great Wall of China in 2013.

Possibly The Coolest Sport Ever! ▶▶▶

Trampolines are awesome fun. Dodgeball is a popular playground game. Put them together and you've got one of the coolest sports ever!

Sports Kids!

Here's our annual salute to kids making waves in the sports world.

Sam Gordon: Thanks to the Internet and her own amazing football skills, Sam Gordon became a star. She was only 9 when she gained 1,911 yards in her pee-wee football league in Utah. Video of her tackle-breaking runs went viral. She got her picture on a Wheaties box and the NFL invited her to the Super Bowl!

Judd Henkes: Shaun White . . . watch your back! By the time he was 10 years old, Judd Henkes was such an awesome snowboarder that he got a sponsorship from a major national sports clothing line. Judd started snowboarding when he was just five. In the years since, he has mastered some of the toughest tricks while practicing at Mammoth Mountain in California. He's done very well in competitions, too. In 2013, he won slopestyle and half-pipe at the national scholastic tournament. He also won the 2012 half-pipe there! Is he a future X Games star?

◀◀◀ Julian Newman: He was only in fifth grade in early 2013, but he played high school basketball in Florida and helped his team win 21 games. His dribbling and passing skills were seen nationwide thanks to YouTube, and Julian appeared on several TV shows. He told Scholastic's *Action Magazine* that he practices six or seven hours a day!

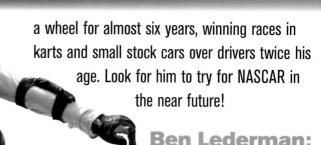

a wheel for almost six years, winning races in karts and small stock cars over drivers twice his age. Look for him to try for NASCAR in the near future!

Ben Lederman:

In 2012, Ben was just 12 when he became the first player from America to be accepted into FC Barcelona's famous soccer academy. He moved from his home near Los Angeles to train and go to school at La Masia. That's where superstar players like Lionel Messi and Andrés Iniesta learned their skills.

Tom Schaar: ▲

This young skateboard hero became the first person ever to land a 1080 in 2012. He's done it again since in competition. Not bad for a guy who won't turn 15 until 2014.

Conner and Cayden Long: ▶▶▶

Conner is a great all-around athlete who excels at triathlons. He runs, bikes, and swims in long races. His younger brother Cayden comes along with him, even though Cayden has cerebral palsy and can't walk on his own. Conner pushes or pulls a trailer and even pulls a raft in the swimming part of the races. The inspirational boys were named the 2012 SportsKids of the Year by *Sports Illustrated Kids* magazine.

Blake Jones:
He turned 16 in 2013 and got his driver's license. But Blake has been behind

Mega-Awesome Sports Internet List!

MAJOR SPORTS WEBSITES

These are the "Big Five" of professional sports leagues. Each of these websites includes links to the individual websites of the teams in the league, plus bios of top players, video clips, schedules of games, even how to find tickets!

Major League Baseball
mlb.com

National Football League
nfl.com

National Basketball Association
nba.com
wnba.com

Major League Soccer
mlssoccer.com

National Hockey League
nhl.com

Editor's Note for Parents and Teachers: These websites are for information purposes only and are not an endorsement of any program or organization over others. We've made every effort to include only websites that are appropriate for young sports fans, but the Internet is an ever-changing environment. There's no substitute for adult supervision, and we encourage everyone to surf smart . . . and safe!

OTHER SPORTS LEAGUES

Check out these websites for schedules, results, and info on athletes in your favorite sports featuring individual competitors.

Action Sports
allisports.com

Bowling
pba.com

Drag Racing
nhra.com

Golf
pgatour.com
lpga.com

Ice Skating
usfigure
skating.org

IndyCar Racing
indycar.com

**Motocross/
Supercross**
supercross.com

Stock Car Racing
nascar.com

Surfing
aspworldtour.com

Tennis
atpworldtour.com
wtatennis.com

COLLEGE SPORTS

Follow your favorite team's road to the football BCS championship or the basketball Final Four with these major college sports sites. You can find links to the schools that are members of these conferences.

**Bowl Championship
Series**
bcsfootball.org

Atlantic Coast Conference
theacc.com

Big East Conference
bigeast.org

Big Ten Conference
bigten.org

Big 12 Conference
big12sports.com

Conference USA
conferenceusa
.com

Mid-American Conference
mac-sports.com

**Mountain West
Conference**
themwc.com

Pac-12 Conference
pac-12.com

**Southeastern
Conference**
secdigitalnetwork
.com

Sun Belt Conference
sunbeltsports.org

**Western Athletic
Conference**
wacsports.com

**National Collegiate
Athletic Association**
ncaa.com
This site features information about all the college sports championships at every level and division.

MAJOR SPORTS EVENTS

You'll find links to most big-time events—like the Super Bowl, the World Series, or the NBA Finals—on those sports' league websites. But here are several more world-wide sporting events that are worth a bookmark.

Little League World Series
littleleague.org/world-series/index.html

The Masters
masters.com

Tour de France
letour.fr/us

Winter Olympics (2014)
sochi2014.com

Summer Olympics (2016)
rio2016.org.br/en

World Cup Soccer (2014)
fifa.com

Women's World Cup Soccer (2015)
fifa.com/womensworldcup/index.html

World Baseball Classic
worldbaseballclassic.com

X Games
espn.go.com/action/xgames

YOUTH SPORTS ORGANIZATIONS

Rather play than watch? These websites can help get you out on the field!

Baseball
littleleague.org

Basketball
njbl.org

Football
usafootball.com

Golf
juniorlinks.com

Ice Hockey
usajuniorhockey.com

Soccer
ayso.org

Tennis
usta.com

MEDIA SITES

If you're looking for the latest scores or news about your favorite sport, try some of these websites run by sports cable channels or sports publications.

CBS Sports
cbssports.com

ESPN
espn.go.com

FOX Sports
msn.foxsports.com

Sporting News Magazine
sportingnews.com

Yahoo! Sports
sports.yahoo.com

SPORTS HISTORY

It seems like big fans know all there is to know about the history of their favorite sports. Learn more about yours at any of these websites that take you back in time.

Hickok Sports
hickoksports.com

Retrosheet (Baseball)
retrosheet.org

***Sports Illustrated* Vault**
sportsillustrated
.cnn.com/vault

Sports Reference Family of Sites
baseball-reference.com

basketball-reference.com

pro-football-reference.com

hockey-reference.com

sports-reference
.com/olympics

PLAYERS ASSOCIATIONS

You're probably a little young to think about making money playing a sport. But if you're interested in the business side of things or want to discover more about what it's like to be a pro athlete, these sites may help.

MLB Players Association
mlbplayers
.mlb.com

NBA Players Association
nbpa.org

NFL Players Association
nflplayers.com

NHL Players Association
nhlpa.com

MLS Players Union
mlsplayers.org

GAMES

Finally, check out these sites for some rainy-day sports fun and games on the computer.

nflrush.com

sikids.com

Big Events 2013-14

September 2013

1 Cycling
Mountain Bike World Championships, final day, Pietermaritzburg, South Africa

5 Football
NFL regular season begins

8–9 Tennis
U.S. Open final matches, New York, New York

16–22 Wrestling
World Championships, Budapest, Hungary

19–22 Golf
Tour Championship, PGA Atlanta, Georgia

19 Basketball
WNBA playoffs begin

October 2013

1–6 Golf
Presidents' Cup, Dublin, Ohio

1 Baseball
MLB postseason begins (Wild Card playoff games, League Division Series, League Championship Series, World Series)

12 Swim/Bike/Run
Ironman Triathlon World Championship, Hawaii

November 2013

3 Running
New York City Marathon

17 Stock Car Racing
Ford Ecoboost 400, final race of NASCAR Chase for the Cup, Homestead, Florida

December 2013

5–8 Rodeo
National Finals Rodeo, Las Vegas, Nevada

7 College Football
ACC Championship Game, Charlotte, North Carolina

Big Ten Championship Game, Indianapolis, Indiana

SEC Championship Game, Atlanta, Georgia

Pac-12 Championship Game, Site TBD

7 Soccer
MLS Cup, Site TBD

6, 8 College Soccer
Women's College Cup, Cary, North Carolina

14, 15 College Soccer
Men's College Cup, Philadelphia, Pennsylvania

January 2014

1 College Football
Rose Bowl, Pasadena, California
Orange Bowl, Miami, Florida
Heart of Dallas Bowl, Dallas, Texas
Gator Bowl, Jacksonville, Florida
Capital One Bowl, Orlando, Florida
Fiesta Bowl, Glendale, Arizona

2 College Football
Sugar Bowl, New Orleans, Louisiana

3 College Football
Orange Bowl, Miami, Florida

4–5 NFL
Wild Card Playoff Weekend

5–12 Figure Skating
U.S. Figure Skating Championships, Boston, Massachusetts

6 College Football
Bowl Championship Series National Championship Game, Pasadena, California

11–12 Football
NFL Divisional Playoff Weekend

19 Football
NFL Conference Championship Games

23–26 Action Sports
Winter X Games 18, Aspen, Colorado

25-26 Tennis
Australian Open finals

26 Football
AFC-NFC Pro Bowl, Honolulu, Hawaii

February 2014

2 Football
Super Bowl XLVIII, East Rutherford, New Jersey

TBA* Baseball
Caribbean Series, Margarita Island, Venezuela

7–23 Winter Olympics
Sochi, Russia

16 Basketball
NBA All-Star Game, New Orleans, Louisiana

23 Stock Car Racing
(NASCAR) Daytona 500, Daytona Beach, Florida

March 2014

19–21 Action Sports
Winter X Games Europe, Tignes, France

24–30 Figure Skating
World Figure Skating Championships, Saitima, Japan

TBA* Hockey
NHL playoffs begin

April 2014

5–7 College Basketball
NCAA Men's Final Four, Arlington, Texas

6–8 **College Basketball**
NCAA Women's Final Four,
Nashville, Tennessee

10–13 **Golf**
The Masters, Augusta, Georgia

May 2014

3 **Horse Racing**
Kentucky Derby, Churchill
Downs, Louisville, Kentucky

8–10 **Football**
NFL Draft,
New York, New York

15–18 **Action Sports**
Summer X Games
Austin, Texas

17 **Horse Racing**
Preakness Stakes, Pimlico
Race Course, Baltimore,
Maryland

17 **Soccer**
FA Cup Final match,
London, England

25 **IndyCar Racing**
Indianapolis 500, Indianapolis,
Indiana

June 2014

7 **Horse Racing**
Belmont Stakes, Belmont Park,
Elmont, New York

7–8 **Tennis**
French Open, final matches,
Paris, France

12–15 **Golf**
U.S. Open Championship,
Pinehurst, North Carolina

12 **Soccer**
World Cup begins,
Brazil

13 **College Baseball**
College World Series begins,
Omaha, Nebraska

TBD **Basketball**
NBA Finals, Site TBD

19–22 **Golf**
U.S. Women's Open,
Pinehurst, North Carolina

July 2014

5 **Cycling**
Tour de France begins,
York, England

5–6 **Tennis**
Wimbledon Championships
finals, London, England

13 **Soccer**
World Cup Final,
Rio de Janeiro, Brazil

15 **Baseball**
MLB All-Star Game,
Minneapolis, Minnesota

17 **Swimming**
World Championships,
Kazan, Russia (end Aug. 2)

17–20 **Golf**
British Open Championship,
Liverpool, England

TBA* **Soccer**
MLS All-Star Game,
Portland, Oregon

August 2014

TBA* **Baseball**
Little League World Series,
Williamsport, Pennsylvania
(throughout month)

7–10 **Golf**
PGA Championship,
Louisville, Kentucky

14–17 **Golf**
LPGA Championship,
Pittsford, New York

21–24 **Gymnastics**
U.S. Gymnastics
Championships,
Pittsburgh, Pennysylvania

As they were in 2010 when Spain won, the eyes of the world will be on the World Cup final on July 13, 2014. The game will be played in Rio de Janeiro, Brazil.

Note: Dates and sites subject to change. *TBA: To be announced. Actual dates of event not available at press time.

Winter Olympic History

In February 2014, the 22nd Winter Olympic Games kick off in Sochi, Russia. Here's a look back at some key stats and details from Winter Games history.

YEAR	LOCATION	YEAR	LOCATION
2014	Sochi, Russia	1968	Grenoble, France
2010	Vancouver, Canada	1964	Innsbruck, Austria
2006	Turin, Italy	1960	Squaw Valley, Idaho, USA
2002	Salt Lake City, Utah	1956	Cortina d'Ampezzo, Italy
1998	Nagano, Japan	1952	Oslo, Norway
1994	Lillehammer, Norway	1948	St. Moritz, Switzerland
1992	Albertville, France	1936	Garmisch-Partenkirchen, Germany
1988	Calgary, Canada		
1984	Sarajevo, Yugoslavia	1932	Lake Placid, New York, USA
1980	Lake Placid, New York, USA	1928	St. Moritz, Switzerland
1976	Innsbruck, Austria	1924	Chamonix, France
1972	Sapporo, Japan		

(1940, 1944: No Winter Games due to World War II.)

WINTER OLYMPICS FACTS

* Until 1994, the Winter Games were held in the same year as the Summer Games. Since then, they have been held two years apart, each on its own every-four-years cycle.

* In 2010, 82 nations were represented, the most ever at a Winter Games.

* With 12 medals, including eight gold, Norwegian cross-country skier Bjorn Dahle is the most-decorated Winter Olympian. In second is another Norwegian, biathlete Ole Einar Bjorndalen with 11.

* Speed skater Apolo Anton Ohno is the top U.S. medal winner in the Winter Games. He earned eight medals. Bonnie Blair, also a speedskater, won six.

* The Southern Hemisphere has never been the site of a Winter Olympics.

World Cup

Billions of people will tune in to parts of the World Cup of soccer in summer 2014. Since the first World Cup in 1930, the event has rivaled the Olympics for world popularity. It's certainly bigger than the Winter Olympics, so here's some background on the biggest sports event you'll watch this year!

ALL-TIME WORLD CUP RESULTS

YEAR	SITE	CHAMPION	RUNNER-UP
2010	SOUTH AFRICA	**Spain**	Netherlands
2006	GERMANY	**Italy**	France
2002	JAPAN/KOREA	**Brazil**	Germany
1998	FRANCE	**France**	Brazil
1994	USA	**Brazil**	Italy
1990	ITALY	**Germany**	Argentina
1986	MEXICO	**Argentina**	West Germany
1982	SPAIN	**Italy**	West Germany
1978	ARGENTINA	**Argentina**	Netherlands
1974	GERMANY	**Germany**	Netherlands
1970	MEXICO	**Brazil**	Italy
1966	ENGLAND	**England**	West Germany
1962	CHILE	**Brazil**	Czechoslovakia
1958	SWEDEN	**Brazil**	Sweden
1954	SWITZERLAND	**West Germany**	Hungary
1950	BRAZIL	**Italy**	Hungary
1938	FRANCE	**Italy**	Hungary
1934	ITALY	**Italy**	Czechoslovakia
1930	URUGUAY	**Uruguay**	Argentina

Note: World Cup was not played in 1942 and 1946 due to World War II.

Produced by Shoreline Publishing Group LLC

Santa Barbara, California

www.shorelinepublishing.com

President/Editorial Director: James Buckley, Jr.

Designed by Tom Carling, www.carlingdesign.com

The *Scholastic Year in Sports* text was written by

James Buckley, Jr.

plus **Beth Craig Zachary** (NHL)

Thanks to Marisa Polansky, Kelly Smith, Annie McDonnell, Steve Diamond, Deborah Kurosz, and the all-stars at Scholastic for all their gold-medal-winning help!

Photo research was done by the authors. Thanks to Scholastic Picture Services for their assistance in obtaining the photos.

● ●

Photography Credits

AP Images: 50 (Andy Manis), back cover, 80 (Cal Sport Media), 84 (Charlie Neibergall), 156 (Charlie Riedel), cover top right (Damian Strohmeyer), cover bottom center (Danny Johnston), 174 (David J. Phillip), cover bottom left (Duane Burleson), 49 (John Miller), 128 (Phillip Abbott), 58-59 (Matt Slocum), 73 (Matt York), 178 (Phelan M. Ebenhack), 130 bottom (Rick Scuteri), 131 (Teresa Long), 109 (Nathan Denette), 70 (Chip Litherland), 39 (Tomasso DeRosa), 176-177 (Vincent Thian), 100, 179 top

Corbis Images/Rick Osentoski: cover bottom right

Courtesy of SkyZone: 179 bottom

Getty Images: cover top left, 26, 147, 152 (Al Bello), 181 top (Alex Grimm), 168 (Alexis Boichard), 90, 95 (Andrew D. Bernstein), 37 (Andy King), 36, 83 bottom (Andy Lyons), 7 center, 12 (Anja Niedringhaus), 60 (Baltimore Sun), back cover (Barry Gossage), 32 (Boston Globe), 7 center right (Bruce Bennett), 13 (Bruce Bennett), 20-21, 76-77, 119 top, 121 top, 124-125 (Chris Graythen), 86 (Chris Jones), 7 bottom left, 14-15, 171 (Christian Petersen), 161 (Clive Brunskill), 127 bottom (Clive Mason), 182 right, 183 top, 183 center, 183 bottom right, 184 top left (Comstock), 184 top center (Comstock), 184 top right, 184 bottom left (Comstock), 184 bottom right (Comstock), 107 (Dave Sandford), 134 -135 (David Ramos), 163 (Dennis Grombkowski), 24, 173 top (Doug Pensinger), 172 (Drew Hallowell), 82 (Eddie Murray), 22-23, 72 (Ezra Shaw), 118 (Fred Vuich), 169 (Geoff Robins), 173 bottom (George Burns), 108 (Grant Halverson), 30, 155 (Gregory Shamus), 5 (Hannah Foslien), 7 center left, 11, 33, 34, 142 (Harry How), 85 (Hartford Courant), 136, 137 (Heuler Andrey), 157 (Isaac Brekken), 145 (Jaime Reina), 110 (Jamie Sabau), 116 (Jared C. Tilton), 65, 67 (Jason O. Watson), 189 (Javier Soriano), 71 bottom (Jay Biggerstaff), 139 (Jean-Pierre Clatot), 69 (Jeff Gross), 130 top (Jeff Kardas), 97 (Jeff Zelevansky), 7 bottom center, 16-17 (Jesse D. Garrabrant), 7 top right, 10 (Jim Davis), 63, 91, 94 (Jim McIsaac), 79 (Joe Robbins), 120 botttom (John Harrelson), 7 bottom right (John Iacono), 18 -19 (John Iacono), 181 bottom (John Sciulli), 7 top center, 9 (John Sleezer), 106 (John Tlumacki), 102-103, 141, 51 (Jonathan Daniel), 44 (Jonathan Ferrey), 105 (Jonathan Kozub), 98 (Jordan Johnson), 138, 160 (Julian Finney), 52 (Justin Aller), 68 (Kansas City Star), 27, 46, 47, 48, 88 -89, 93 (Kevin C. Cox), 7 top left, 8 (Leon Halip), 64 (Mark Cunningham), 55 (Miami Herald), 78, 99 (Michael Hickey), 144 (Michael Regan), 29 (Mike Ehrmann), 175 (Mike Hewitt), 71 top (Mike Stobe), 166-167 (Mitchell Gunn), 62 (Mitchell Layton), 127 top (Nelson Almeida), 121 bottom (Nick Laham), 140 (Patricia de Melo Moreira), 111 (Patrick McDermott), 163 (Paul Crock), 45 (Peter G. Aiken), 182 left, 183 bottom left, 185 top, 185 bottom (PhotoDisc), 83 top (Pool), 126 (Rainer W. Schlegelmilch), 162 (Rindoff), 28, 35 (Rob Carr), 170 (Rob Carr), 129 (Robert Laberge), 38, 66 (Ron Vesely), 92 (Ronald Martinez), 154 (Ross Kinnaird), 120 top (Scott Halleran), 104 (Scott Levy), 180 (Stephen M. Dowell/Orlando Sentinel), 149 (Steve Dykes), 42-43, 96 (Streeter Lecka), 54 (Thearon Henderson), 119 bottom (Tom Whitmore), 114-115 (Tyler Barrick), 146 (VI Image), 148 (Victor Decolongon), 81 (Wichita Eagle)

Shutterstock, Inc.: cover background;

USA TODAY Sports Images/Kevin Jairaj: 53.